WHO Technical Report Series

914

THE SELECTION AND USE OF ESSENTIAL MEDICINES

Report of the WHO Expert Committee, 2002
(including the 12th Model List of Essential Medicines)

World Health Organization

Geneva 2003

WHO Library Cataloguing-in-Publication Data

WHO Expert Committee on the Selection and Use of Essential Medicines
(12th : 2002 : Geneva, Switzerland)
The selection and use of essential medicines : report of the WHO Expert Committee,
2002 : (including the 12th model list of essential medicines).

(WHO technical report series ; 914)

1.Essential drugs — standards   2.Formularies — standards
3.Drug information services — organization and administration   4.Drug utilization   5.Guidelines
I.Title   II.Title: 12th model list of essential medicines   III. Series.

ISBN 92 4 120914 3   (LC/NLM classification: QV 55)
ISSN 0512-3054

Typeset in Hong Kong
Printed in Singapore
2002/14862 — SNPBest-set/SNP — 7000

Contents

WHO Expert Committee on the Selection and Use of Essential Medicines
Geneva, 15–19 April 2002

Members*

Professor P.M. de Buschiazzo, Department of Pharmacology, School of Medicine, University of La Plata, La Plata, Argentina (*Co-chairperson*)

Professor T. Fukui, Department of General Medicine and Clinical Epidemiology, Kyoto University Graduate School of Medicine, Kyoto, Japan

Professor A. Helali, Director, Centre National de Pharmacovigilance et Matériovigilance, Ministère de la Santé et de la Population, Algiers, Algeria

Professor R. Laing, Boston University School of Public Health, Boston, MA, USA (*Co-rapporteur*)

Professor J.-R. Laporte, Director, Fundacio Institut Català de Farmacologia, Department of Pharmacology and Therapeutics, Universitat Autonoma de Barcelona, Barcelona, Spain (*Co-chairperson*)

Professor D. Ofori-Adjei, Director, Noguchi Memorial Institute for Medical Research, University of Ghana, Accra, Ghana

Dr E.M.A. Ombaka, Coordinator, Eucumenical Pharmaceutical Network, World Council of Churches, Nairobi, Kenya

Professor M.M. Reidenberg, Chief, Division of Clinical Pharmacology, The New York Hospital – Cornell Medical Centre, New York, NY, USA

Professor S. Suryawati, Director, Centre for Clinical Pharmacology and Drug Policy Studies, Gadjah Mada University, Yogyakarta, Indonesia (*Co-rapporteur*)

Dr L. Wannmacher, Department of Clinical Pharmacology, School of Medicine, University of Passo Fundo, Rio Grande do Sul, Brazil

Representatives of other organizations[†,‡]

Joint United Nations Programme on HIV/AIDS (UNAIDS)
Dr C. Michon, Care Adviser, UNAIDS, Geneva, Switzerland

United Nations Children's Fund (UNICEF)
Ms Thuy Huong Ha, Supply Division, UNICEF, Copenhagen, Denmark

WHO Collaborating Centre for Drug Statistics Methodology
Ms M. Rønning, WHO Collaborating Centre for Drug Statistics Methodology, Oslo, Norway

---

* Each Member of the Committee signed a statement that he or she agreed not to participate in the review of any matter under consideration in which there was a real or perceived conflict of interest. Two Members reported an interest but no real or perceived conflicts of interest were disclosed.

† Unable to attend: The World Bank and the United Nations Population Fund (UNFPA).

‡ Each representative of other organizations signed a statement that he or she agreed not to participate in the review of any matter under consideration in which there was a real or perceived conflict of interest. One representative reported an interest but no real or perceived conflicts of interest were disclosed.

WHO Collaborating Centre for International Drug Monitoring (Uppsala, Sweden)
Professor C.J. van Boxtel, Professor of Clinical Pharmacology, Amsterdam, Netherlands

Secretariat*

Dr R.C.F. Gray, Medical Officer, Policy, Access and Rational Use, Department of Essential Drugs and Medicines Policy, WHO, Geneva, Switzerland

Professor D. Henry, Medical Officer, Policy, Access and Rational Use, Department of Essential Drugs and Medicines Policy, WHO, Geneva, Switzerland (*Temporary Adviser*)

Dr S. Hill, Faculty of Health, University of Newcastle, Waratah, NSW, Australia (*Temporary Adviser*)

Dr H.V. Hogerzeil, Coordinator, Policy, Access and Rational Use, Department of Essential Drugs and Medicines Policy, WHO, Geneva, Switzerland (*Secretary*)

Professor J.M. Makinde, Head, Department of Pharmacology and Therapeutics, University of Ibidan, Ibidan, Nigeria (*Temporary Adviser*)

Mr D.K. Mehta, Executive Editor, *British national formulary*, Royal Pharmaceutical Society, London, England (*Temporary Adviser*)

Dr P. Mugyenyi, Joint Clinical Research Centre, Kampala, Uganda (*Temporary Adviser*)

Dr S.L. Nightingale, Department of Health and Human Services, Washington, DC, USA (*Temporary Adviser*)

Dr S. Sharma, Delhi Society for the Promotion of Rational Use of Drugs, New Delhi, India (*Temporary Adviser*)

Dr K. Weerasuriya, Regional Adviser, Essential Drugs and Medicines Policy, WHO Regional Office for South-East Asia, New Delhi, India

Mr P.J. Wiffen, Coordinating Editor, *Pain, Palliative and Supportive Care*, Cochrane Collaborative Review Group, Pain Research Unit, Churchill Hospital, Oxford, England (*Temporary Adviser*)

---

* Each Temporary Adviser of the Committee signed a statement that he or she agreed not to participate in the review of any matter under consideration in which there was a real or perceived conflict of interest. No real or perceived conflicts of interest were disclosed.

1. Introduction

The WHO Expert Committee on the Use of Essential Drugs met in Geneva from 15 to 19 April 2002. The meeting was opened on behalf of the Director-General by Dr J. Quick, Director, Department of Essential Drugs and Medicines Policy, who drew attention to the fact that 2002 was the twenty-fifth anniversary of the WHO Model List of Essential Drugs (the Model List). He mentioned that this was an especially significant meeting, not only because it would be the first to operate under new procedures but also because it would be required to discuss several important issues, such as the application for the inclusion in the Model List of a number of antiretroviral medicines for the treatment of human immunodeficiency virus/acquired immunodeficiency syndrome (HIV/AIDS). The Committee would also be required to report to the Director-General on progress in the implementation of the new procedures and to suggest future improvements.

The Secretary informed participants that following a request from the WHO Secretariat, the Committee had agreed to hold an open session as part of its present meeting (see section 2). The reason for the open session was to allow all stakeholders to participate in discussions and to comment on issues relating to the WHO Model List of Essential Drugs. For Expert Committee members, it created an opportunity to receive first-hand additional information and opinions on matters under consideration. Participants were assured that the discussions and considerations of the open session would be reflected in the report of the meeting. A summary of the Committee's meeting report would be submitted to the WHO Executive Board in January 2003, together with a statement on the public health implications of its recommendations.

In a change from the format adopted for previous reports, the Committee decided to present the updated version of the Model List (the 12th) as an annex to its meeting report (Annex 1). In addition to a full set of explanatory notes, Annex 1 provides background information relating to the development and use of the Model List. Supporting evidence for the safety and efficacy of those medicines that were recommended for inclusion at the present meeting is summarized in Annex 2.

2. Open session

The open session was opened by Dr Y. Suzuki, Executive Director, Health Technology and Pharmaceuticals, who stated that this meeting should be seen in the light of other related activities, such as the recent publication of the first list of pre-qualified products and suppliers of medicines for the treatment of HIV/AIDS (*1*). He reminded participants that all their comments would be noted and that final recommendations on each of the agenda items would be formulated in subsequent private sessions of the Committee.

3. The new procedures for updating and disseminating the Model List

3.1 Background

At its previous meeting held in 1999, the Committee reviewed past experience with the Model List and discussed future needs (*2*). It noted that:

— with regard to the selection process for essential medicines, efforts to link the selection of medicines for inclusion in the Model List to WHO treatment guidelines should be further encouraged;
— decisions on whether or not to include medicines in the Model List should be based on properly identified evidence, and the reasons for their inclusion or otherwise should be carefully recorded;
— proposals to include medicines in the Model List need to be better defined, and should include a valid analysis of the cost-effectiveness of each medicine;
— available evidence supporting the inclusion of medicines already on the Model List should be identified and made available;
— more explicit criteria for determining which diseases or conditions should be covered by the Model List are required, as are clearer descriptions of the criteria for selecting medicines for inclusion in the Model List;
— the Model List should not only identify priority conditions and those medicines for which equitable availability and affordability should be ensured before resources are spent on other treatments (i.e. a "core" list of essential medicines), but should also indicate medicines that are cost-effective and safe but which are not necessarily affordable and/or for which special training or health care services would be needed for their proper use (i.e. a "complementary" list of essential medicines).

On the basis of these discussions, the Committee recommended that the methodology for its decision-making be reviewed as a matter of some urgency. It was agreed that, following such a review, a methodology for use by the Committee at its subsequent meetings should be prepared and that this methodology should include a description of the process for submitting a proposal to include a medicine in the Model List (2).

In May 2001, an information document proposing a timetable for developing new procedures for updating the Model List was presented to the Executive Board at its 108th session (3). In June 2001, Member States were invited to comment on a discussion paper, "Updating and disseminating the WHO Model List of Essential Drugs: the way forward" (4). Once comments from Member States had been taken into account, a revised version of the discussion paper was sent out for wider review in August 2001, this time to Member States, WHO collaborating centres, members of expert advisory panels, organizations of the United Nations system, nongovernmental organizations, professional associations, national essential medicines programmes, universities, representatives of the pharmaceutical industry and patients' organizations. Over 140 comments were received in response to the circulation of the paper.

The proposals for revising the procedures were discussed at the Forty-third Directing Council of the Pan American Health Organization (the Fifty-third Session of the WHO Regional Committee for the Americas) in September 2001. Participants raised a number of concerns and constructive comments were duly noted. The proposals were also discussed at the Forty-eighth Session of the WHO Regional Committee for the Eastern Mediterranean in October 2001, which strongly endorsed, by resolution EM/RC48/R.2, the proposed new procedures for updating the WHO Model List and requested the Director-General to finalize them as soon as possible (5).

3.2 Key features of the new procedures

As a result of the above two-stage consultation process, new procedures for updating and disseminating the Model List have been drawn up. The main features of the new procedures are as follows:

— the use of the term "essential medicines" instead of "essential drugs" to reflect the common use of the term "medicines" to describe pharmaceutical preparations used in clinical health care practice;

— a more systematic approach to inviting and dealing with applications for medicines to be included in, or deleted from, the Model List;

— a more transparent process for selecting medicines for inclusion in the Model List, including a systematic analysis of the evidence that supports the medicines proposed for use in the care of different health conditions (e.g. comparative evidence of efficacy, safety and, where possible and appropriate, cost-effectiveness);

- opportunities for interested parties to comment on both the application and its review to the Expert Committee;
- full involvement of different WHO departments in the application and selection process, and in the linking of the process to clinical guidelines published and disseminated by WHO;
- development of a new WHO Essential Medicines Library which facilitates access to information about medicines on the Model List (see section 3.5);
- steps to ensure that the Expert Committee operates with full scientific independence as it makes its final recommendations (in line with current practice for decisions on regulatory approval, procurement and reimbursement of medicines within Member States).

The new procedures were presented in a report by the WHO Secretariat (6) at the 109th session of the WHO Executive Board in January 2002 and discussed. The Board noted the report, including the attached Annex that sets out the new procedures (7). The Director-General decided to organize the next meeting of the Expert Committee on the Use of Essential Drugs in April 2002, taking into account the above-mentioned discussions on the new procedures while recognizing the fact that, owing to the relatively short time frame involved, not all of the proposed improvements could be implemented immediately.

3.3 Review of the new procedures

As a prelude to further discussion, a presentation was made during the open session to inform participants about progress in formulating the new procedures for updating and disseminating the Model List. In general, there was wide support for the move from experience-based to evidence-based decisions, for the increased link between selection and evidence-based clinical guidelines and for the establishment of the WHO Essential Medicines Library. While recognizing the fact that not all aspects of the new procedures could be implemented in time for the present meeting, it was considered that practical experience gained during the course of this meeting, the first to use the new procedures, should be evaluated carefully in order to make recommendations to the Director-General for future refinement of the procedures.

3.3.1 Applications for additions

The new procedures state that all applications for additions to the Model List should be submitted through the appropriate WHO technical department, i.e. the department that deals with the disease or condition pertaining to the medicine in question. During the open session, concern was expressed that some WHO departments might not be able or willing to process applications, or that some diseases, such as neglected diseases, might not be covered by a WHO technical department. It was suggested that an additional procedure would be needed for filing applications in such cases.

In its discussion of the new procedures that followed the open session, the Expert Committee acknowledged that a separate mechanism was required for applications that are not submitted by an appropriate WHO technical department, or for which no relevant technical department exists within WHO. The Committee therefore recommended that the new procedures should allow any individual or organization, including technical departments within WHO, to submit an application. Applications should always be submitted directly to the Secretariat of the Expert Committee, who, after reviewing the application for completeness, should send any outside application to the relevant WHO department for detailed consideration. External authorities would be consulted in the event that the disease or condition in question was not covered by a WHO department. If the Secretariat, preferably after consultation with the relevant WHO department, concluded that the application was inappropriate for review by the Expert Committee or did not follow the standard format for applications and/or failed to provide the necessary information, a provisional decision not to proceed with the application could be taken. A provisional decision, along with the application and supporting documentation, should be reported to the Expert Committee at its next meeting for final endorsement.

The Committee also recommended that the new standard review procedure for applications for additions to the Model List should be modified as shown in Table 1.

3.3.2 *Applications for deletions*

At the open session a number of participants expressed their support for a survey of medicines on national lists of essential medicines as a means of identifying potential medicines for deletion from the WHO Model List, with those medicines appearing on only a few national lists qualifying as candidates for deletion. A simplified review process for medicines proposed for deletion was also suggested. Proposals for deletion could be posted on the WHO web site and comments invited. If no positive arguments for maintaining the medicine on the Model List were submitted, it could be deleted at the next session of the Committee after due consideration of the available evidence. It was

Table 1

Standard review procedure for an application to include an item in the Model List[a]

Steps of the procedure	Web[b]
1. The application is submitted to the Secretariat of the Expert Committee.	X
2. The Secretariat of the Expert Committee:	
i) checks whether the application is complete;	
ii) logs receipt of the application;	X
iii) forwards the application, together with any supporting documentation to the appropriate WHO technical department or WHO Collaborating Centre (i.e. the "Assessor");	
iv) posts a summary of the application on the WHO web site for general comment;	X
v) monitors the progress of the application.	
3. The Assessor nominates an expert, preferably a member of the Expert Committee, to oversee the assessment of the application and to become the "Presenter".	X
4. On the basis of his/her preliminary assessment, the Assessor makes a recommendation either:	X
i) not to proceed with further assessment; or	
ii) to proceed with a full assessment.	
5. In the case of a full assessment, the Assessor:	
i) conducts a search for evidence relevant to the application;	X
ii) assesses data on comparative efficacy, safety and cost-effectiveness;	
iii) formulates a summary and a draft recommendation to the Expert Committee;	
iv) when inclusion of a medicine in the Model List is recommended, provides information on:	
— the individuals for whom the medicine will be used;	
— the conditions in which the medicine will be used;	
— the circumstances in which the medicine will be used, the dose, formulation, strength, route of administration, duration of treatment and details of the monitoring required;	
— whether the medicine should be included in the core or complementary list;	
— whether any other medicine should be removed from the Model List.	
6. On completion of the full assessment, the Secretariat posts the results and the draft recommendation on the WHO web site for comment.	X
7. Draft text for inclusion in the *WHO model formulary* is drawn up and posted on the WHO web site for comment.	X
8. At the next meeting of the Expert Committee, the Presenter outlines the Assessor's recommendation regarding the medicine in question and the evidence supporting its inclusion or otherwise in the Model List.	
9. The Expert Committee decides whether to accept the Assessor's recommendation and comments on the draft version of the text to be included in the *WHO model formulary*.	
10. The Model List and *WHO model formulary* are updated according to the recommendations of the Expert Committee.	X

[a] Replaces the standard review procedure as given in Box 2, Annex 1 of document EB109/8 (7).

[b] An X in this column indicates that the step or the relevant information should be posted on the WHO web site.

felt that this approach would not only encourage active participation in the new procedures for updating the Model List but would also allow WHO to devote its resources to the systematic review of medicines proposed for inclusion.

During the open session, several participants submitted proposals for the deletion or review of medicines on the Model List. The comment was made that as many of the medicines on the Model List are frequently registered for over-the-counter use, medicines should only be deleted after a careful review of all the available information.

In its discussions, the Committee acknowledged that the new procedures for handling applications for additions to the Model List were not particularly well suited to dealing with deletions from the Model List, and that separate procedures for this purpose were required. The Committee recommended that decisions to delete an item from the Model List should, as far as possible, be evidence-based while recognizing the fact that evidence from clinical trials may not always be available for some of the older medicines on the Model List. The Committee recommended separate procedures for applications for deletions made by the Expert Committee (i.e. Committee-initiated applications) and those made by other organizations and individuals (i.e. other applications).

Committee applications for deletion
Applications to delete items from the Model List might be initiated by the Committee in the following cases:

— if a medicine has been superseded by other products in terms of efficacy, safety or cost-effectiveness;
— if drug regulatory authorities have withdrawn the medicine, usually for reasons of safety;
— if new WHO clinical guidelines have been published that no longer recommend the medicine;
— if the medicine is rarely used or purchased from international suppliers such as the United Nations Children's Fund (UNICEF).

In such cases, details of the medicine(s) proposed for deletion, together with a statement of the reasons for the deletion and supporting evidence, should be posted on the WHO web site, whenever possible at least 6 months in advance of the next meeting of the Committee. In its assessment of the medicine proposed for deletion, the Committee would take into account all comments and any additional data received in response to the proposal.

Other applications for deletion

Applications to delete an item from the Model List may be made by any organization or individual and would be expected to occur in the following circumstances:

— within the context of a systematic review of a therapeutic group of medicines;
— in relation to an application for inclusion of another product;
— on the basis of experiences of significant concerns about safety or efficacy arising from use in different settings.

In the case of applicant-led proposals, an application for deletion should be submitted to the Secretariat of the Expert Committee; the application should contain a review of data on efficacy and safety and any other relevant evidence. This information would be posted on the WHO web site for comment. At its next meeting, the Committee would consider the application for deletion and any comments received as a result of the circulation of the proposal.

3.3.3 Selection criteria

During the open session, a number of participants commented on the criteria used to select medicines for inclusion in the Model List, in particular, with regard to fixed-dose combination products. It was noted that fixed-dose combinations offer certain advantages; they facilitate adherence to treatment regimens and they can delay the emergence of antimicrobial resistance. It was also noted that many illogical and ad hoc combinations of various medicines are currently being marketed in a number of countries. Any proposal to include fixed-dose combinations in the Model List should be backed by adequate proof of pharmaceutical compatibility and bioavailability.

In light of these comments, the Committee recognized that its selection criteria with regard to fixed-dose combination products were in need of review and recommended that they be modified as follows:

> Most essential medicines should be formulated as single compounds. Fixed-dose combination products should be selected only when the combination has a proven advantage in therapeutic effect, safety, adherence or in decreasing the emergence of drug resistance in malaria, tuberculosis and HIV/AIDS.

3.4 The WHO model formulary

At its meeting in 1995, the Committee recommended that WHO develop a model formulary to complement the Model List and to act as a useful resource for countries wishing to develop their own national formulary (8). It was envisaged that such a model formulary would be updated every 2 years.

The Committee was informed of progress in the development of the *WHO model formulary*. Following a series of consultations (held in 1996, 1997 and 1999), the first draft had been completed at the end of 1999. In early 2000, it was agreed that the Royal Pharmaceutical Society of Great Britain (which, together with the British Medical Association, publishes the *British national formulary*) would take responsibility for checking and finalizing the first edition of the *WHO model formulary*.

As part of the editorial process, all statements in the draft text were compared with the original references and checked for consistency with other WHO documents and recommendations, and against reputable drug information sources, including published regulatory information. A full record of this data validation exercise and all ensuing technical and editorial changes to the draft text, together with the underlying reasons for the changes and all relevant references, is available. When necessary, the text was updated to take into account new information that had become available since the time of the original drafting. In addition, monographs were included for the small number of essential medicines that had been added to the Model List at the meeting of the Committee held in November 1999 (*2*).

Although the initial intention was to maintain the section headings and numbering system of the Model List, this proved difficult in practice, largely because the sections of the Model List are not always useful as therapeutic categories and do not easily lend themselves to introductory evaluative statements. Small changes were therefore introduced. The *WHO model formulary* has also been generous in repeating the formulary text of those essential medicines that are listed under more than one therapeutic category. The lack of full concurrence with the numbering system of the Model List should not present a major problem. Users of the *WHO model formulary* will be able to access the information they require either through its contents list or through the main index (which includes both medicine names and disease terms).

The *WHO model formulary* will be made available in various electronic formats, including CD-ROM and via the Internet through the WHO Essential Medicines Library web site. The latter will contain electronic links to the Model List. The electronic version of the *WHO model formulary* is intended to serve as a starting point for countries and institutions wishing to develop their own formularies. National or institutional formulary committees can adapt the *WHO model formulary* to suit their own needs by altering the existing text or by aligning the *WHO model formulary* to their own list of essential medicines by adding or deleting entries.

At the time of the present meeting (April 2002), the first edition of the *WHO model formulary* was in its final stages of editing; electronic versions were expected to become available during 2002 (*9*). The Committee noted that the first draft of the *WHO model formulary* had been based on the 10th Model List (i.e. as revised in 1997) but had since been updated so as to be consistent with the 11th Model List (i.e. as revised in 1999). The Committee recommended that the *WHO model formulary* be further updated to reflect those changes made to the Model List by the Committee at its present meeting prior to its publication in final form.

Following a request from the WHO Secretariat, the Committee also recommended that Appendix 3 of the *WHO model formulary* concerning the suitability of medicines for use by breastfeeding mothers be updated, as it was based on an out-dated 1995 WHO publication, *Breastfeeding and maternal medication* (*10*).

It was not possible for the Committee to review the proposed formulary text for those medicines for which applications for inclusion in the Model List had been received at the present meeting (as required by the new procedures) owing to time constraints. However, the Committee recognized the evolving role of the *WHO model formulary* in relation to the Model List, and the need for countries to consider both when developing their own lists of essential medicines.

3.5 The WHO Essential Medicines Library

Since 1975, WHO has received repeated requests from the World Health Assembly for information on the quality, price and therapeutic aspects of individual pharmaceutical products included in the Model List. At its previous meeting in 1999, the Expert Committee stressed the importance of the links between the selection of medicines for the Model List, medicines information and clinical treatment guidelines (*2*). It also supported the suggestion that there should be wider dissemination of the evidence used by the Committee in the course of its work and recommended the careful recording of the reasons for its final recommendations regarding the inclusion or otherwise of medicines in the Model List.

The new procedures for updating and disseminating the Model List include the creation, by WHO, of an electronic Essential Medicines Library to make information about essential medicines more widely available using CD-ROMs and the Internet (see section 3.2). Within the latter, links to WHO clinical guidelines, the *WHO model formulary*, existing United Nations price information services and information on international nomenclature and quality standards are envisaged.

The Committee was informed of progress in the preparation of the Essential Medicines Library. The database structure has been created and the Model List entered, together with brief summaries of the reasons for the inclusion of each medicine and key references to systematic reviews. Summaries of WHO clinical guidelines are being finalized and electronic links to the *WHO model formulary* are under development. The aim is to launch the Essential Medicines Library web site in late 2002, and to continue to add other components of the library as and when they become available. An overview of the structure of the Essential Medicines Library, showing the main external partners, is given in Figure 1.

The Expert Committee expressed its satisfaction with the progress achieved to date, and agreed that all available means of disseminating the information in the WHO Essential Medicines Library should be explored and encouraged, including for example, CD-ROMs and Internet downloads to national centres for local dissemination. Specific electronic files could be provided on request to the WHO's Department of Essential Drugs and Medicines Policy.[1]

With regard to the content of the Essential Medicines Library, the Committee recommended that details of the applications for the addition to the Model List of all new medicines should be maintained on the library web site (as part of the presentation of the underlying evidence for their inclusion), as well as records of the Committee's decisions and archival files for items that have been considered at previous meetings.

The Committee noted that most of the information under the Essential Medicines Library umbrella was held in external data sources that were outside its control and responsibility. However, in this regard it wished to make an exception for the text of the *WHO model formulary* for newly added medicines. Although not formally approved by the Committee, the *WHO model formulary* had been initiated as a result of a recommendation made by the Committee and several of its members had been involved in the project. Furthermore, the *WHO model formulary* is a natural repository for information the Committee might wish to make available when making its recommendations

---

[1] Requests for information should be addressed to the Department of Essential Drugs and Medicines Policy, World Health Organization, 1211 Geneva 27, Switzerland.

Figure 1
The Essential Medicines Library

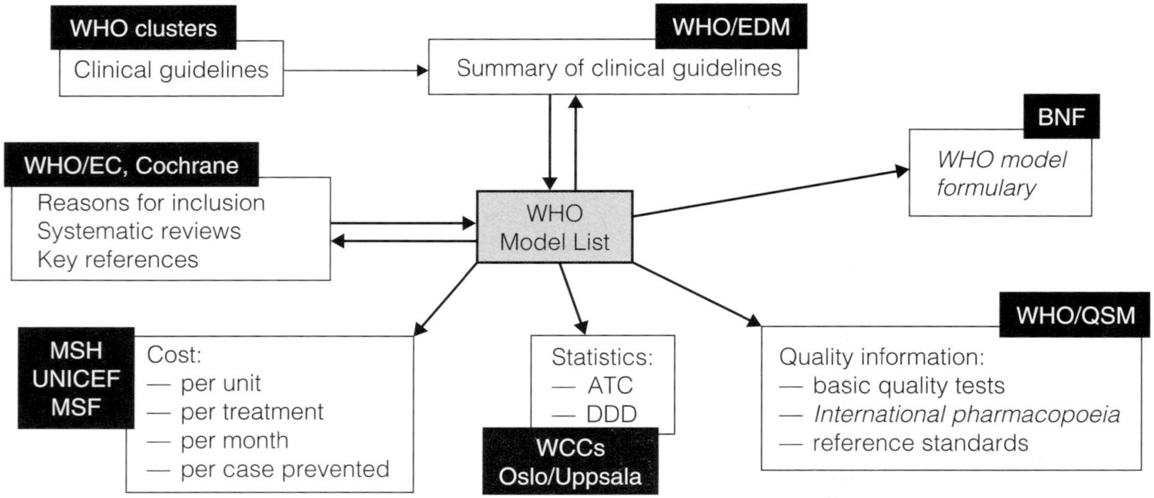

ATC, Anatomical Therapeutic Chemical classification; BNF, British National Formulary; DDD, Defined Daily Dose; MSH, Management Sciences for Health; MSF, Médecins sans Frontières; WCC, WHO Collaborating Centre; WHO/EC, WHO Expert Committee on the Selection and Use of Essential Medicines; WHO/EDM, WHO Department of Essential Drugs and Medicines Policy; WHO/QSM, Quality and Safety (Medicines) team of WHO/EDM on the inclusion of medicines in the Model List. For these reasons, the Committee endorsed the requirement in the new procedures that the text of the *WHO model formulary* monograph for a new medicine should be considered by the Committee at the same time as its application for inclusion in the Model List.

The Committee recommended that key sections of the Essential Medicines Library be made available in languages other than English. To this end, it recommended that WHO should consider the feasibility and potential benefits of creating Internet hot-links to appropriate information sites in other languages, and to the web sites of well established drug regulatory agencies. Review articles appearing in independent publications could be included in the systematic review process for medicines proposed for inclusion.

4. Other outstanding technical issues

4.1 Change of name of the Expert Committee

The first Expert Committee, convened in 1977 was called the "WHO Expert Committee on the Selection of Essential Drugs" and its meeting report, *The selection of essential drugs. Report of a WHO Expert Committee (11)*. These names were retained by the Committee at its second meeting in 1979 (*12*). In 1982, at its third meeting, the Committee changed its name and thereafter was referred to as the "WHO Expert Committee on the Use of Essential Drugs" and its meeting report was called, *The use of essential drugs. Report of a WHO Expert Committee (13)*.

When developing the new procedures for updating and disseminating the Model List during 2001 (see section 3.1), WHO started to use the term "essential medicines" as an alternative to "essential drugs". The reasons for the change are as follows:

- The term "medicines" is more commonly used to describe pharmaceutical preparations used in clinical health care practice.
- For non-native English speakers, the word "drugs" is frequently associated with narcotic or illicit substances (i.e. hard drugs). Consequently, it is not always clear what is meant by a "national drug policy".
- In other languages, for example in French and Spanish, this ambiguity does not exist: "médicaments essentials" and "medicamentos esenciales" are already widely accepted official terms.
- 2002 is not only the 25-year anniversary of the Model List but also sees the launch of the WHO Essential Medicines Library; both of

these milestones create a timely opportunity to introduce new names.

At its present meeting, the Committee recognized that the main focus of its activities is to advise on the selection of essential medicines. However, selection cannot be separated from use, as evidenced by the development of stronger links with standard clinical guidelines and the creation of the WHO Essential Medicines Library. The Committee also considered that it would be useful for WHO to maintain an expert forum to review recent developments in rational drug use.

In light of the above considerations, the Committee recommended to change its name from the "WHO Expert Committee on the Use of Essential Drugs" to the "WHO Expert Committee on the Selection and Use of Essential Medicines".

4.2 Description of essential medicines

In 1975, the World Health Assembly by resolution WHA28.66 requested the Director-General to advise Member States on "the selection and procurement, at reasonable cost, of essential drugs of established quality corresponding to their national health needs" (*14*). Subsequently, in 1978, resolution WHA31.32 stressed "the need to provide essential drugs of adequate quality, in sufficient quantity and at reasonable cost to meet the health needs of countries", and endorsed the aim of, "ensuring access of the whole population to essential drugs at a cost the country can afford" (*15*).

At its first meeting held in 1977, the WHO Expert Committee on the Selection of Essential Drugs described essential drugs as medicines that "are of utmost importance, and are basic, indispensable and necessary for the health needs of the population" (*11*). In 1982, at its third meeting, the Expert Committee modified the description of essential drugs to, "those that satisfy the health care needs of the majority of the population; they should therefore be available at all times in adequate amounts and in the appropriate dosage forms" (*13*). This description was endorsed and used at all subsequent meetings of the Committee, up until its meeting in 1999.

At its meeting held in 1999, the Committee decided to combine this description with the affordability concept from resolution WHA31.32, and stated that, "Essential drugs are those that satisfy the health care needs of the majority of the population; they should therefore be available at all times in adequate amounts and in the appropriate dosage forms, and at a price that individuals and the community can afford" (*2*). This was the description that was used in the information paper submitted to the Executive Board in May 2001 (see section 3.1) (*3*).

Most reviewers who took part in the 2001 review of the proposals for new procedures for updating the Model List (see section 3.1) expressed their satisfaction with the description of essential medicines that was agreed in 1999. However, some reviewers questioned the inclusion of the phrase on affordability while others had reservations about the expression, "the majority of the population". In addition, there were concerns that the need for sustained financing for essential medicines and the need for essential medicines of adequate quality, were not adequately reflected in the description.

In its report to the Executive Board of January 2002 (*6*), the WHO Secretariat stated that the description of essential medicines should include three components: a definition, a description of the selection criteria and a description of the purpose for which such a list is developed, as follows:

- *Definition.* Essential medicines are those that satisfy the priority health care needs of the population.
- *Selection criteria.* Essential medicines are selected with due regard to disease prevalence, evidence on efficacy and safety, and comparative cost-effectiveness.
- *Purpose.* Essential medicines are intended to be available within the context of functioning health systems at all times in adequate amounts, in the appropriate dosage forms, with assured quality, and at a price the individual and the community can afford.

This description is similar to that formulated at the first meeting of the Expert Committee in 1977, i.e. essential medicines are those that "are of utmost importance, and are basic, indispensable and necessary for the health needs of the population" (*11*). The purpose of the Model List was articulated by the Committee at its third meeting held in 1982 in the statement, "they should therefore be available at all times in adequate amounts and in the appropriate dosage forms" (*13*). A combination of the definition and its implications has been used to describe the essential medicines concept at all subsequent meetings of the Committee.

The WHO Secretariat in its report to the Executive Board (2001) highlighted one further element that hitherto had not been reflected in the descriptions of essential medicines used to date, namely the need for countries and institutions to develop their own list of essential medicines. As stated by the Expert Committee at its meeting in 1999, "the concept of essential drugs . . . is intended to be flexible and adaptable to many different situations; exactly which drugs are regarded as essential remains a national responsibility" (2).

The open session provided the Committee with a further opportunity to seek opinions about the wording of the description of essential medicines. It was noted that the current phrasing states that essential medicines are selected, "with due regard to disease prevalence, evidence on efficacy and safety, and comparative cost-effectiveness. However, several participants felt that the term "disease prevalence" did not cover the use of preventive medicines and items for family planning and therefore suggested that the aspect of prevention be added to the "selection criteria" part of the description.

The Committee endorsed the suggestion made during the open session regarding the wording of the description of essential medicines and thus recommended the replacement of "disease prevalence" by "public health relevance" in the section on selection criteria, and the addition of "with adequate information" to the section on purpose and "implementation of" to the last sentence. With these amendments, the full description would read as follows:

> Essential medicines are those that satisfy the priority health care needs of the population. They are selected with due regard to public health relevance, evidence on efficacy and safety, and comparative cost-effectiveness. Essential medicines are intended to be available within the context of functioning health systems at all times in adequate amounts, in the appropriate dosage forms, with assured quality and adequate information, and at a price the individual and the community can afford. The implementation of the concept of essential medicines is intended to be flexible and adaptable to many different situations; exactly which medicines are regarded as essential remains a national responsibility.

4.3 Role of treatment costs in relation to the Model List

The cost of medicines has been a matter of specific concern to Member States since the concepts of national drug policies and essential medicines were first introduced in 1975 (11, 14–16). Questions about the use of cost and cost-effectiveness information in the selection of essential medicines were also raised by several reviewers who took part in the 2001 consultation process (section 3.1), including:

— whether the high cost of a medicine could prevent its inclusion in the Model List even if it satisfied the selection criteria on grounds of need (i.e. it was needed to treat a priority health problem), effectiveness (when compared with other medicines used to treat the same condition) and safety;

— whether worldwide comparisons of the cost-effectiveness of different medicines in treating specific conditions would be meaningful, given the wide cost variations and the dynamic nature of prices for the same medicine.

During the open session, it was stressed that price information needs to be collected and used with care and that price information can quickly become out of date. It was recognized that for the selection of essential medicines only indicative price information is needed, with a focus on price comparisons within therapeutic categories. In addition, the comment was made that information about current prices is not always easy to obtain.

With regard to the selection criteria, the new procedures specify that:

— the absolute cost of a medicine will not be a reason to exclude it from the Model List if it meets the stated selection criteria;
— cost-effectiveness comparisons must be made among medicines within the same therapeutic group (e.g. for identifying the most cost-effective medicine treatment to prevent mother-to-child transmission of HIV).

This approach is in line with WHO's practice of including cost considerations in the development of public health recommendations.

The Committee noted that the impact of cost variations on estimates of cost-effectiveness could be addressed through the use of information on indicative prices of medicines that are already available within the United Nations system, and through the rigorous identification of sources of cost information. Where available, cost-effectiveness analyses and systematic reviews could also be used. The Committee expressed its hope that, with time, Member States' experiences in using cost-effectiveness analysis would lead to further refinements and improvements in the new procedures.

4.4 Inclusion of additional items in the Model List

The Model List currently contains a variety of items, such as vaccines, diagnostic agents and chemicals, sera, immunoglobulins, and various non-medicine items such as condoms, insect repellents and other preventive equipment. The Committee acknowledged that the inclusion of these additional items opened the door to many more applications of this nature (e.g. impregnated bednets) which, in turn, could lead to much additional work in areas where personal preferences dominate and objective evidence on which to base comparisons is relatively scarce.

As a general principle, the Committee recommended that any item that is normally subject to regulatory control could be considered for inclusion in the Model List. Such items would typically be subject to clinical studies on efficacy and safety, the results of which the Committee considered that it had the necessary expertise to assess. Items that enter the human body, such as radio contrast media and other invasive diagnostic tests, intrauterine devices, vaccines, sera and immunoglobulins, would come under this category. Several other items, which have long been included, such as condoms, should probably be maintained on the Model List. However, for new applications it was considered that a more pragmatic approach was needed. The Committee thus recommended that a separate mechanism with appropriate procedures be established to identify and assess essential medical devices and health technologies.

A request to create an active web link within the Essential Medicines Library to information on HIV/AIDS diagnostic test kits was referred back to the WHO Secretariat for consideration. With regard to vaccines, the Committee agreed to a proposal put forward by the Department of Vaccines and Biologicals, WHO, that the latter, through its Advisory Committees and a transparent review process, would synthesize its current recommendations on vaccines into a format that is compatible with the Model List of Essential Medicines. This draft list of vaccines, together with relevant supporting evidence, would be forwarded to the Committee for consideration for adoption as part of the Model List. The Committee recommended that the core children's vaccines, as well as vaccine combinations, should be included in this systematic review.

The Committee noted that the misuse of injections is a serious and widespread problem that demands interventions at several levels. In situations of high injection use, the use of injectable medications needs to be reduced through the development and promotion of clinical guidelines and through the training of health professionals and consumers. When injectable medications are being supplied, the necessary equipment for sterile injections should also be provided.

5. Format and presentation of the 12th Model List

5.1 Section headings

At present, medicines on the Model List are listed alphabetically under 27 main therapeutic use categories. Although this system of sectioning may not have the rigour of alternative systems, for example, the Anatomical Therapeutic Chemical (ATC) classification in which medicines are divided into different groups according to the organ or system on which they act (*17*), it is widely used by supply agencies and for national lists of essential medicines. Any decision to change the current system of section headings and/or numberings in the Model List should therefore be taken with great care.

At its present meeting, the Committee considered promoting and adopting the ATC classification for the Model List, but concluded that, although the ATC system was not only widely supported and promoted by WHO but was also gaining acceptance as a global classification system, its adoption would only be acceptable if essential information about the classification was freely available in the public domain. Currently, this is not the case. The Committee also noted that information relating to the 5-level ATC code number for each item in the Model List is probably less relevant than the logic of the classification system itself. The Committee thus recommended not to add the ATC code numbers to the Model List itself, but to list separately the items on the Model List with their corresponding 5-level ATC code numbers (see Annex 3). This approach would allow a gradual introduction of the ATC system and leave international organizations, such as UNICEF, with the option to maintain the old system or to change to the ATC classification. The Committee also recommended that WHO should actively pursue ways and means of putting the relevant information on the ATC system in the public domain.

5.2 The core and complementary lists

Traditionally, the Model List has contained three categories of medicines:

— medicines on the main list;
— medicines designated as "complementary" for any one of three reasons (i.e. if medicines in the main list cannot be made available; if medicines in the main list are known to be ineffective or inappropriate for a given individual; or if the medicine is for use in rare disorders or in exceptional circumstances);
— medicines for restricted indications.

With time, the distinctions between these categories have become blurred; nor has the categorization always been applied systematically. Nevertheless, despite the wide disparity in national needs and resources, clearly defined categories of essential medicines are widely regarded as being useful for promoting the global concept of priority setting in health care.

The opinions of Model List users regarding the categorization of essential medicines were sought as part of the 2001 consultation process (see section 3.1). The consensus view that emerged was that there was no need for a separate category for "medicines for restricted indications" (as the Committee's comments on their use would not only be noted in the Model List itself but would also be recorded in the Committee's report and thus become part of the Essential Medicines Library), but that the distinction between core and complementary medicines should be maintained. At the present meeting, the Committee endorsed the proposal to maintain the core and complementary listings, at least for the time being, and recommended that the two lists be presented separately (Annex 1).

The current version of the Model List thus makes the following distinction between core and complementary list medicines:

- *The core list*: presents a list of minimum medicine needs for a basic health care system, listing the most efficacious, safe and cost-effective medicines for priority conditions. Priority conditions are selected on the basis of current and estimated future public health relevance, and potential for safe and cost-effective treatment.
- *The complementary list*: presents essential medicines for priority diseases which are efficacious, safe and cost-effective but not necessarily affordable, or for which specialized health care facilities or services may be needed.

The Committee noted that the new description of the complementary list and the call for greater consistency in its application implied that the designation of all items currently on the Model List would need to be reviewed (see also section 7.2).

5.3 The "square box" symbol

The square box symbol indicates that a listed medicine should be seen as a representative example from a group of clinically equivalent medicines (within a pharmacological class) with wide experience of use. The medicine listed on the Model List is intended to be the least costly therapeutic equivalent within the group. National lists should not use a similar symbol and should be specific in their final selection, which would depend on local availability and price.

The Committee considered that, in view of the relatively large number of items on the Model List that currently carry the square box symbol, a review of its use should be initiated (see also section 7.3).

6. Changes made in revising the Model List

Proposals for amendments to the Model List, including applications for additions and deletions, received by the Committee for consideration at its present meeting are summarized below.

6.1 Applications for additions

6.1.1 Antiretroviral medicines

Applications for the addition of 12 antiretroviral (ARV) medicines to the Model List were received from the WHO Department of HIV/AIDS. All of the proposed medicines are recommended for use as antiretroviral medicine combinations in the new WHO clinical guidelines for antiretroviral treatment in resource-poor settings (*18*).

In accordance with the new procedures (see section 3.3), the Committee reviewed written submissions containing information about the 12 medicines; these submissions comprised summaries of available evidence relating to clinical benefits and adverse effects, practical details of treatment, and comparisons with other members of their therapeutic group. The clinical evidence had been assembled from comprehensive literature reviews for each medicine and medicine combination, several of which had been conducted by staff working for the Cochrane Collaboration. The written submissions also provided background information on the public health impact of HIV infection worldwide, the overall impact of ARV therapy on the course of illness in HIV-infected subjects, the value of surrogate markers as measures of treatment response, and a summary of the experience and impacts of delivering ARV therapy in resource-limited settings.[1]

The content of the written submissions was summarized for members of the Committee in a series of oral presentations made by WHO staff from the Departments of HIV/AIDS and Essential Drugs and Medicines Policy. Presentations were also given on the history of the development of WHO guidelines for the use of ARVs in resource-limited settings and on recent experience with ARVs in selected developing countries. Issues such as the rationale for the selection of first-line and alternative regimens, the development of appropriate criteria for case selection, and minimum standards for monitoring treatment response and toxicity were of particular interest and concern to the Committee.

---

[1] The full application is available from the WHO Essential Medicines Library via the Internet at http://mednet3.who.int/mf/.

Having considered the data before it, the Expert Committee agreed that there was substantive evidence to support the claims of efficacy of ARV combinations comprising three or four medicines. Such combinations typically comprise two nucleoside reverse transcriptase inhibitors (NRTIs) given in conjunction with either a non-nucleoside reverse transcriptase inhibitor (NNRTI), or a third NRTI, or a protease inhibitor. The Committee accepted the validity of surrogate markers of efficacy (i.e. CD4 cell counts and viral load estimates), which had been used in the majority of clinical trials of these agents. The Committee also agreed that both meta-analyses of randomized clinical trials and large, well conducted cohort studies provided convincing evidence that combination ARV treatment substantially reduces AIDS mortality. Furthermore, survival gains were not seen to be offset by severe adverse effects. It was thus concluded that effective ARV treatment leads to large absolute reductions in mortality and the restoration of a worthwhile quality of life. However, highly active ARV therapy is not a cure for HIV/AIDS and long-term suppressive therapy is necessary.

Before considering each individual application, the Committee raised a number of issues that were of general concern. These were:

— the need for listing what was seen to be a large number of medicines;
— the safety and efficacy of therapy when delivered with the minimal levels of laboratory monitoring advocated in the WHO clinical guidelines;
— the advantages and disadvantages of fixed-dose combinations.

The first, the large number of medicines proposed for listing, was addressed by staff from the Department of HIV/AIDS. The point was made that while there are many circumstances where one essential medicine may substitute readily for other members of its class, thus allowing the placement of a single agent on the Model List (with appropriate advice about substitution), this is not possible in the case of HIV treatment. Effective therapy requires commencement of at least three medicines simultaneously, and alternative regimens are necessary to meet specific requirements at start-up, to substitute for first-line regimens in the case of toxicity, or to replace failing regimens. The Committee thus agreed that if the ARV agents were to be listed, then all of the proposed medicines should be added to the Model List.

The availability of adequate laboratory monitoring of ARV therapy was a particular concern of several members of the Committee. The current WHO ARV guidelines allow a relatively low level of monitoring, i.e. a level that can be provided by basically equipped health facilities (*18*). This raises questions about the safety of ARV therapy, in particular, concerns that an inability to recognize medicine toxicity and/or failing regimens could, in turn, lead to viral resistance. It was noted that not many large field studies have been conducted on the efficacy and safety of ARV therapy provided under such circumstances. Following extensive debate, the Expert Committee agreed to accept the current WHO clinical guidelines regarding case selection and monitoring. However, the Committee recommended that these issues should be reviewed at its next meeting, that suitable footnotes should be added to specific medicines in the Model List, and that appropriate organizations should be strongly encouraged to fund field trials of low-level monitoring of ARV treatments. The Committee also supported the proposal that laboratory facilities for CD4 counts should be made available more widely and encouraged the Global Fund to Fight AIDS, Tuberculosis and Malaria to support the provision of such services.

The advantages and disadvantages of prescribing fixed-dose combinations of ARV medicines were also discussed. The principal advantage of fixed-dose combinations is the improved adherence to treatment due to simplification of regimens, which in turn should result in higher levels of efficacy and lower rates of viral resistance. The main disadvantages are inflexibility in dosing, and doubts about the pharmaceutical quality of fixed-dose combination products that are produced in the absence of strict regulatory and quality standards. In principle, the Committee was in favour of assured quality fixed-dose combination products that incorporate suitable doses of appropriate medicine combinations. It was noted that, at present, only a limited number of such combinations are available internationally. However, it is likely that the availability of fixed-dose combinations will increase in the future and it is hoped that the relevant products will be tested under the WHO's pre-qualification programme as soon as is practicable.

When considering each individual medicine proposed for listing, the Committee took the following materials into account:

— the written application for each medicine (some of which had been available on the WHO web site prior to the meeting);
— any additional written material received from external stakeholders;
— oral presentations (also provided in hard copy) by staff from WHO and the Joint United Nations Programme on HIV/AIDS (UNAIDS).

Generally speaking, the evidence contained in the applications was classified as follows:

- Level 1. Evidence from relevant high quality systematic reviews of unbiased randomized comparative clinical trials.
- Level 2. Evidence from at least one relevant unbiased randomized comparative clinical trial.
- Level 3. Evidence from relevant controlled observational studies.

A summary of the supporting evidence for each application is provided in Annex 2.

The Committee also debated whether the medicines should be included in the core or in the complementary section of the Model List. It was argued that complementary listing could be used to signal that, to date, experience of the use of ARV therapy in resource-poor settings was limited. On the other hand, it was felt that complementary listing would be inconsistent with previous decisions regarding medicines that require monitoring and, moreover, the decision might be used inappropriately as an argument against wider access to ARV medicines. On balance, concerns about the problems of limited laboratory monitoring notwithstanding, the Committee decided that core listing was appropriate, with the addition of suitable footnotes.

In sum, the Committee recommended that the following medicines be added to the core section of the Model List:

— the nucleoside reverse transcriptase inhibitors, zidovudine (ZDV or AZT), lamivudine (3TC), stavudine (d4T), didanosine (ddI) and abacavir (ABC);
— the non-nucleoside reverse transcriptase inhibitors, nevirapine (NVP) and efavirenz (EFV or EFZ);
— the protease inhibitors, nelfinavir (NFV), indinavir (IDV), lopinavir/low-dose ritonavir (LPV/r), ritonavir(r) and saquinavir (SQV).

The Committee also requested that the following notes be added to the Model List:

The antiretroviral medicines do not cure the HIV infection, they only temporarily suppress viral replication and improve symptoms. They have various adverse effects and patients receiving these medicines require careful monitoring by adequately trained health professionals. For these reasons, continued rigorous promotion of measures to prevent new infections is essential and the need for this has not been diminished in any way by the addition of antiretroviral medicines to the Model List. Adequate resources and trained health professionals are a prerequisite for the introduction of this class of medicines. Effective therapy requires commencement of three or four medicines simultaneously, and alternative regimens are necessary to meet specific requirements at start-up, to substitute for first-line regimens in the case of toxicity, or to replace failing regimens. The Committee strongly recommends the use of three- or four-medicine combinations as specifically recommended in the WHO clinical guidelines (*18*). The use of fixed-dose preparations for these combinations is also recommended, with assured pharmaceutical quality and inter-changeability with the single products as approved by the relevant drug regulatory authority.

Selection of two or three protease inhibitors from the Model List will need to be determined by each country after consideration of local clinical guidelines and experience, as well as the comparative costs of available products. Ritonavir is recommended for use in combination with indinavir, lopinavir and saquinavir as a booster, and not as a medicine in its own right.

It was noted that the current WHO ARV guidelines recommend the use of the total lymphocyte count as a surrogate for a CD4 count only for HIV-infected individuals who were, or had been, symptomatic (*18*). It was requested that the permanent copies of the submissions for the ARV medicines be amended to reflect this.

6.1.2 *Artemether + lumefantrine (fixed-dose combination)*

The first application to include the antimalarial, artemether + lumefantrine, in the Model List was reviewed by the Committee at its previous meeting in 1999 (*2*). At that time, the Committee considered that, although the fixed-dose combination had the potential to play an important role in the management of uncomplicated falciparum malaria, it was not appropriate to include it in the Model List for the following reasons:

— there were no data on the operational use of the combination;
— two dosage regimens had been proposed by the manufacturer, one for use in non-immune patients and one for use in semi-immune patients, which might lead to confusion;
— concerns regarding the degree of compliance that may be obtained in rural health settings with a medicine combination that required a relatively long and complex treatment regimen (i.e. 6 doses over 60 hours);
— the affordability of the combination for populations in greatest need.

At its present meeting, the Committee considered a revised application.[1] The Committee noted that the prevalence of drug-resistant falciparum malaria has increased to the extent that, in some countries, resistance to all of the available antimalarial medicines, except artemisinin and its derivatives (including artemether), exists. For patients with falciparum malaria resistant to chloroquine, mefloquine, quinine and sulfadoxine + pyrimethamine, the use of artemisinin and its derivatives is considered essential.

---

[1] The full application is available from the WHO Essential Medicines Library via the Internet at http://mednet3.who.int/mf/.

The Committee also appreciated the pricing arrangements that have been made by the manufacturer, which have led to a long-standing agreement for a differential price for developing countries (relative to developed countries) as well as an agreed price differential within developing countries between the private sector, the public sector and not-for-profit health care systems. Products destined for these three markets are distinguished by different names and packaging.

The Committee noted that a recommendation to include artemisinin combinations would, in the medium term, necessitate a review of the need to maintain the single artemisinin derivatives that are currently on the Model List. The Committee concluded that it would be premature to delete these medicines at the present time and recommended that single artemisinin and its derivatives be retained on the 12th Model List but reserved for severe cases of malaria in situations were there is resistance to quinine.

Despite the absence of detailed clinical data on the use of artemether + lumefantrine in children below 10 kg and limited information on its use in pregnancy, the Committee recommended the addition of artemether + lumefantrine to the core section of the Model List, with the following footnote:

> Recommended for use in areas with significant drug resistance and not in pregnancy or in children below 10 kg.

The Committee encouraged the development of new fixed-dose combinations of artemisinin as well as long-acting antimalarial medicines for future comparative review.

The evidence used to support the application to include artemether + lumefantrine in the Model List is summarized in Annex 2.

6.1.3 α/β-Arteether

The Committee reviewed the application for the inclusion of the antimalarial, α/β-arteether.[1] It considered that there was insufficient evidence to prove a comparative advantage in efficacy or safety when compared with other medicines in its therapeutic class, and insufficient published information on experience of its use in a variety of settings. The Committee also noted that the Roll Back Malaria programme did not recommend its inclusion for the same reasons. The Committee therefore decided not to recommend the addition of α/β-arteether to the Model List.

---

[1] The full application is available from the WHO Essential Medicines Library via the Internet at http://mednet3.who.int/mf/.

6.1.4 *Artemotil (β-arteether)*

The Committee reviewed the application for the inclusion of artemotil (β-arteether), another antimalarial.[1] In considering the evidence before it, the Committee noted that the observations made for α/β-arteether also applied to artemotil; in addition, artemotil was not registered for use in adults. On these grounds, the Committee recommended not to include artemotil in the Model List.

6.1.5 *Amodiaquine*

The Committee reviewed the application for the inclusion of the antimalarial, amodiaquine.[2] Amodiaquine was included in the first Model List drawn up in 1977 (*11*), but was removed in 1979 (*12*), reinstated in 1982 (*13*) and removed again in 1988 (*19*) in view of safety concerns in prophylactic use. The Committee was encouraged by new evidence regarding the efficacy and cost-effectiveness of amodiaquine in areas with resistance to chloroquine and sulfadoxine + pyrimethamine contained in the present application. However, it noted with concern the results of a trial of amodiaquine in children which suggested that use of the medicine might be associated with high rates of neutropenia. Potentially useful pharmacovigilance data from other sources, such as studies on the use of amodiaquine in treated populations, were not supplied.

In view of the above, and the fact that amodiaquine had been removed twice for safety reasons, the Committee considered that a careful review of safety information was needed before it could decide to add this medicine again to the Model List. The Committee therefore decided to defer its decision to its next meeting, and requested more detailed information about the safety of amodiaquine, in particular, when used for curative purposes in resource-poor settings. The Committee recommended that Member States and national committees take their own decision on the use of amodiaquine in the light of local circumstances and available information.

6.1.6 *Insecticide-treated bednets*

The Committee reviewed an application for the inclusion of insecticide-treated bednets. The Committee, recognizing the public health burden of malaria, acknowledged the need for prevention strategies and the potential role that insecticide-treated bednets could

---

[1] The full application is available from the WHO Essential Medicines Library via the Internet at http://mednet3.who.int/mf/.
[2] The full application, plus a supportive memorandum, is available from the WHO Essential Medicines Library via the Internet at http://mednet3.who.int/mf/.

play in this regard. The Committee noted that many different insecticides were currently being used to treat bednets, that different strategies for their retreatment existed, and that new long-acting products were being developed. The Committee also noted that treated bednets are not usually regulated by national regulatory agencies and, as such, would not normally qualify for inclusion in the Model List (see also section 4.4).

In light of these considerations, the Committee decided to defer its decision regarding the application pending the receipt of evidence on the use and effectiveness of long-acting insecticide-treated bednets. As the issue was raised in the application, the Committee noted that tariffs and taxes can create a considerable burden for equitable access to essential medicines, medical devices and health technologies and recommended that this matter be addressed by WHO.

6.1.7 *Miconazole nitrate buccal tablets*

The Committee reviewed the application for the inclusion of miconazole nitrate buccal tablets[1]. The Committee recognized that miconazole ointment or cream was already on the Model List, as an antifungal medicine (for topical use). The absence of comparative data for miconazole nitrate buccal tablets and nystatin lozenges was of concern to the Committee. It concluded that, as insufficient evidence was presented as to its comparative advantage in efficacy and safety, miconazole nitrate buccal tablets should not be added to the Model List.

6.2 Applications for deletions

No formal applications for deletions from the Model List were received by the Committee.

6.3 Other changes

6.3.1 *Meglumine antimoniate*

The Committee reviewed an application to change the dosage of meglumine antimoniate, an antiprotozoal, from "approximately 8.5%" to "approximately 8.1%". It decided to recommend the change, following the correction made in the Dictionnaire Vidal (*20*).

6.3.2 *Antineoplastic and immunosuppressive medicines*

Pending a full review of the designation of all items on the Model List (see section 7.2), the Committee recommended that all the medicines

---

[1] The full application is available from the WHO Essential Medicines Library via the Internet at http://mednet3.who.int/mf/.

in sections 8.1–8.3 immediately be classed as complementary, because the use of these medicines requires specialized facilities.

6.3.3 *Reserve list medicines*

Pending a full review of the designation of all items on the Model List (see section 7.2), the Committee recommended that all medicines formerly classed as "medicines for restricted indications" be immediately classed as complementary medicines, the "restricted indications" category having been abandoned in the present revision of the Model List (see section 5.2). This change affects various antibacterials, several antimalarials and a group of medicines considered essential for the treatment of multidrug-resistant tuberculosis.

7. Future reviews of sections of the Model List

7.1 Update on the review of medicines for the treatment of hypertension

The Committee was informed of progress in updating the existing clinical guidelines for the treatment of hypertension (*21*) currently being undertaken as a joint project by WHO and the International Society for Hypertension (ISH). The review process is being conducted according to the new WHO procedures on guideline development as approved by the WHO Cabinet in January 2001 (*22*). At the time of the present meeting, the systematic review of the evidence had been completed and the draft report and recommendations were at the peer-review stage. It was anticipated that the revised clinical guidelines would be available in final form by the end of 2002.

The Committee recommended that the relevant medicines on the Model List (e.g. hydralazine, methyldopa, nifedipine and reserpine,) be reviewed as soon as the new clinical guidelines were published. It also recommended that a full review of the other groups of cardiovascular medicines, such as the antiarrhythmic medicines, should be initiated.

7.2 Review of the core and complementary lists

The Committee acknowledged that the new description of complementary list medicines and the need for greater consistency in allocating items to either list (see section 5.2) meant that the designation of all items on the Model List should be reviewed. The suggestion made by some reviewers who took part in the 2001 consultation (see section 3.1) and also by a number of members of the present Committee to abolish all categories of the Model List, replacing them with explanatory notes and/or footnotes appropriate to each item, was noted. The Committee thus recommended that a full review of the placement of all items on the core or complementary lists be undertaken before a final decision is made whether or not to maintain the two separate lists.

7.3 Review of the use of the "square box" symbol

The Committee noted that, at present, a relatively large number of items on the Model List are listed with a square box symbol and recommended that a review be undertaken with a view to restricting its use. In cases where it is decided that the square box symbol should be maintained, the equivalent alternative medicines should be specified.

7.4 Review of injectable medicines

A review of injectable medicines on the Model List was presented.[1] Of the 306 medicines that are currently on the Model List, 135 (44%) are listed as injectable medicines in 173 presentations. Of these, 41 require reconstitution, implying the need for diluents. In view of the problems associated with the use of injections mentioned previously (see section 4.4), the Committee recommended that a review of all injectable medicines on the Model List be carried out. The aim of such a review would be to reduce the total number of medicines listed as injectable forms in favour of other administration routes and/or dosage forms, wherever possible.

7.5 Priorities for further systematic reviews

The Committee considered the various suggestions that had been made at previous meetings regarding the need for systematic reviews of certain sections of the Model List. Referring to recommendations made at the present meeting in connection with the new procedures for deleting items from the Model List (see section 3.3), the Committee also noted that several items on the Model List could probably be deleted without the need for a full review. The Committee recommended that an inventory be made of all suggestions for deletions and/or review of sections of the Model List. On completion of such an inventory, an electronic consultation should be held among members of the Committee and other experts to identify the most urgent items or sections for review. This issue should be raised at the next meeting of the Committee.

---

[1] Available from the WHO Essential Medicines Library via the Internet at http://mednet3.who.int/mf/.

8. Recommendations

8.1 Procedures for updating and disseminating the Model List of Essential Medicines[1]

1. Applications for inclusions, changes or deletions may be submitted to the Secretariat of the Expert Committee on the Selection and Use of Essential Medicines not only by relevant technical departments within WHO but also by any individual or organization.

2. Box 2, the standard review procedure for applications, should be modified, according to the new version provided in the present report of the Expert Committee (see page 6).

3. Specific procedures for deleting an item from the Model List should be developed, with possibilities for either a simplified consultation procedure or a systematic review. In both cases, the evidence for deletion should be carefully recorded.

4. Paragraph 7 on the selection criteria should be amended as follows:

   > Most essential medicines should be formulated as single compounds. Fixed-dose combination products should be selected only when the combination has a proven advantage in therapeutic effect, safety, adherence or in delaying the development of drug resistance in malaria, tuberculosis and HIV/AIDS.

5. The draft *WHO model formulary* should be updated to include the changes made to the Model List in 2002 and published as soon as possible (see Annex 1, Appendix 1).

6. Details of the applications for inclusions, changes or deletions should be maintained on the WHO Essential Medicines Library as part of the presentation of the underlying evidence for the proposed inclusions, changes or deletions. Archival files should be created for all items that have been considered at successive meetings of the Expert Committee.

7. Important sections of the WHO Essential Medicines Library should be made available in languages other than English. In this regard, WHO should consider the feasibility and potential benefits of creating Internet hot-links to reliable information sites in other languages, and to the web sites of well established drug regulatory agencies.

8. Additional resources and capacity should be made available to the WHO Secretariat of the Expert Committee and relevant

---

[1] For a full description of the new procedures for updating and disseminating the Model List of Essential Medicines, please refer to Annex 1 of document EB109/8 (7); this document is also available on the WHO web site at http://www.who.int/medicines.

WHO technical departments to ensure the full implementation of the new procedures.

9. Experiences with the new procedures should be carefully evaluated; this includes those aspects of the procedures that have not yet been implemented in full. When appropriate, the procedures should be further refined.

10. A separate mechanism with appropriate procedures should be created to identify and assess essential medical devices and health technologies.

11. The open session was useful to the work of the Committee, and a similar meeting should be included in the agenda for the next meeting.

8.2 Description of essential medicines

1. The Committee recommended the replacement of the phrase "disease prevalence" by "public health relevance" in the section on selection criteria, the addition of "with adequate information" to the section on purpose, and the addition of "implementation of" to the last sentence of the description of essential medicines.

8.3 Presentation of the 12th Model List

1. The Model List should maintain its current system of section numbering. However, in addition to its usual presentation, the printed version of the Model List should also be presented according to the 5-level Anatomical Therapeutic Chemical (ATC) classification system.

2. WHO should actively pursue ways and means of putting relevant information on the ATC classification in the public domain.

3. The "core" and "complementary" lists should be maintained, but the two lists should be presented separately (see also section 8.7, recommendation 3).

4. The Department of Vaccines and Biologicals, WHO should synthesize its current recommendations on vaccines into a format that is compatible with the Model List of Essential Medicines, and present this summary, with supporting evidence, to the Committee for consideration for adoption as part of the Model List. The EPI vaccines and vaccine combinations should also be included in this systematic review.

8.4 Additions and changes to the Model List

1. The following medicines should be added to the core list of essential medicines under section 6.4.2 (Antiretroviral medicines):

- Nucleoside reverse transcriptase inhibitors: abacavir (ABC), didanosine (ddI), lamivudine (3TC), stavudine (d4T) and zidovudine (ZDV or AZT).
- Non-nucleoside reverse transcriptase inhibitors: efavirenz (EFV or EFZ) and nevirapine (NVP).
- Protease inhibitors: indinavir (IDV), lopinavir/low-dose ritonavir (LPV/r), nelfinavir (NFV), ritonavir (r) and saquinavir (SQV).

The following footnotes should also be added:

> The antiretroviral medicines do not cure the HIV infection, they only temporarily suppress viral replication and improve symptoms. They have various adverse effects and patients receiving these medicines require careful monitoring by adequately trained health professionals. For these reasons, continued rigorous promotion of measures to prevent new infections is essential and the need for this has not been diminished in any way by the addition of antiretroviral medicines to the Model List. Adequate resources and trained health professionals are a prerequisite for the introduction of this class of medicines. Effective therapy requires commencement of three or four medicines simultaneously, and alternative regimens are necessary to meet specific requirements at start-up, to substitute for first-line regimens in the case of toxicity, or to replace failing regimens. The Committee strongly recommends the use of three- or four-medicine combinations as specifically recommended in the WHO clinical guidelines. The use of fixed-dose preparations for these combinations is also recommended, with assured pharmaceutical quality and inter-changeability with the single products as approved by the relevant drug regulatory authority.

> Selection of two or three protease inhibitors from the Model List will need to be determined by each country after consideration of local clinical guidelines and experience, as well as the comparative costs of available products. Ritonavir is recommended for use in combination with indinavir, lopinavir and saquinavir as a booster, and not as a medicine in its own right.

2. Artemether + lumefantrine (fixed-dose combination) should be added to the core list of essential medicines under section 6.5.3a (Antimalarial medicines — for curative treatment).
3. The dosage of meglumine antimoniate should be changed from "approximately 8.5%" to "approximately 8.1%".

8.5 Deferred applications

1. The application to include amodiaquine in the Model List should be deferred pending the receipt of more detailed information on its safety when used for curative purposes in resource-poor settings.
2. The application to include insecticide-treated bednets in the Model List should be deferred pending the receipt of evidence on the use and effectiveness of long-acting products.

8.6 Rejected applications

1. The applications to include α/β-arteether, artemotil and miconazole nitrate buccal tablets in the Model List should be rejected.

8.7 Priorities for future reviews of sections of the Model List

1. Following the updating of the WHO/ISH clinical guidelines for the treatment of hypertension, the section on antihypertensive medicines should be reviewed.
2. A full review of other categories of cardiovascular medicines should be initiated.
3. In view of the new definition of complementary list medicines and the need for greater consistency in its implementation, a full review of the designation of items as either core or complementary list should be undertaken before a decision is made at the next meeting of the Committee whether to maintain the two separate lists.
4. The use of the square box symbol should become more restricted. To this end, a review of the use of the symbol should be undertaken for the next meeting of the Committee.
5. All injectable medicines on the Model List should be reviewed.
6. A full inventory should be made of all other suggestions for deletions and/or review of sections of the Model List. An electronic consultation should be held to identify the most urgent items or sections for future review through one of the two processes recommended in section 8.1, recommendation 3.
7. The glossary which was contained in previous reports of the Committee, should be updated for the next meeting of the Committee.

8.8 Change of name of the Expert Committee

1. The name of the Expert Committee on the Use of Essential Drugs should be changed to the "WHO Expert Committee on the Selection and Use of Essential Medicines".

8.9 Other recommendations

1. The development of appropriate paediatric dosage forms of essential medicines should be encouraged.
2. Tariffs and taxes on essential medicines, medical devices and health technologies create a considerable burden for equitable access to such items. This issue should be addressed by WHO.

Acknowledgements

The Committee recognized the large contribution to the process of evidence-based selection of essential medicines made by the late Professor James Petrie. The Committee expressed its appreciation of the contributions made by staff of the Departments of Essential Drugs and Medicines Policy and HIV/AIDS, the Roll Back Malaria partnership and all other organizations involved in the meeting.

References

1. *Pilot procurement, quality and sourcing project: access to HIV/AIDS drugs and diagnostics of acceptable quality*, 4th ed. Geneva, World Health Organization, 2002 (regularly updated; available from the Internet at http://www.who.int/medicines/organization/par/edl/access-hivdrugs.shtml).

2. *The use of essential drugs. Ninth report of the WHO Expert Committee* (including the revised Model List of Essential Drugs). Geneva, World Health Organization, 2000 (WHO Technical Report Series, No. 895).

3. *Revised procedures for updating the WHO Model List of Essential Drugs: a summary of proposals and process*. Geneva. World Health Organization, 2001 (document EB108/INF.DOC2; available from the Internet at http://www.who.int/gb/).

4. *Updating and disseminating the Model List of Essential Drugs: the way forward*. Geneva, World Health Organization, 2001 (WHO/EDM discussion paper).

5. Resolution EM/RC48/R2. In: *Annual report of the Regional Director for the year 2000 and progress reports. WHO Regional Committee for the Eastern Mediterranean, Forty-eighth Session, Riyadh, Saudi Arabia, October 2001*. Alexandria, WHO Regional Office for the Eastern Mediterranean, 2001.

6. *WHO medicines strategy: revised procedure for updating WHO's Model List of Essential Drugs*. Geneva, World Health Organization, 2002 (document EB109/8; available from the Internet at http://www.who.int/gb/).

7. WHO medicines strategy: procedure to update and disseminate the WHO Model List of Essential Medicines. In: *WHO medicines strategy: revised procedure for updating WHO's Model List of Essential Drugs*. Geneva, World Health Organization, 2002: Annex 1 (document EB109/8; available from the Internet at http://www.who/int/gb/).

8. *The use of essential drugs. Seventh report of the WHO Expert Committee*. Geneva, World Health Organization, 1997 (WHO Technical Report Series, No. 867).

9. *WHO model formulary 2002*. Geneva, World Health Organization, 2002.

10. *Breastfeeding and maternal medication*. Geneva, World Health Organization, 1995 (document WHO/CDR/95.11).

11. *The selection of essential drugs. Report of a WHO Expert Committee*. Geneva, World Health Organization, 1977 (WHO Technical Report Series, No. 615).

12. *The selection of essential drugs. Second report of a WHO Expert Committee.* Geneva, World Health Organization, 1979 (WHO Technical Report Series, No. 641).

13. *The use of essential drugs. Report of a WHO Expert Committee.* Geneva, World Health Organization, 1983 (WHO Technical Report Series, No. 685).

14. WHA28.66. Prophylactic and therapeutic substances. In: *Handbook of resolutions and decisions of the World Health Assembly and the Executive Board, Volume II, 1973–1984.* Geneva, World Health Organization, 1985:129.

15. WHA31.32. Action programme on essential drugs. In: *Handbook of resolutions and decisions of the World Health Assembly and the Executive Board, Volume II, 1973–1984.* Geneva, World Health Organization, 1985:129–130.

16. *Official Record of the World Health Organization,* 226: Annex 13.

17. *Guidelines for ATC classification and DDD assignment,* 2nd ed. Oslo, WHO Collaborating Centre for Drug Statistics Methodology, 1998.

18. *Scaling up antiretroviral therapy in resource-limited settings: guidelines for a public health approach.* Geneva, World Health Organization, 2002 (available on the Internet at http://www.who.int/hiv/topics/arv/ISBN9241545674.pdf).

19. *The use of essential drugs. Model list of essential drugs (fifth list). Third report of the WHO Expert Committee.* Geneva, World Health Organization, 1988 (WHO Technical Report Series, No. 770).

20. *Dictionaire Vidal.* Paris, Editions du Vidal, 1998.

21. *WHO/ISH guidelines for the management of hypertension.* Geneva, World Health Organization, 1999.

22. *Development of WHO treatment guildelines: recommended process.* Geneva, World Health Organization, 2001 (in preparation).

Annex 1
The 12th WHO Model List of Essential Medicines

Introduction

The concept of essential medicines

Essential medicines are those that satisfy the priority health care needs of the population. They are selected with due regard to public health relevance, evidence on efficacy and safety, and comparative cost-effectiveness. Essential medicines are intended to be available within the context of functioning health systems at all times in adequate amounts, in the appropriate dosage forms, with assured quality and adequate information, and at a price the individual and the community can afford. The implementation of the concept of essential medicines is intended to be flexible and adaptable to many different situations; exactly which medicines are regarded as essential remains a national responsibility. Experience has shown that careful selection of a limited range of essential medicines results in a higher quality of care, better management of medicines (including improved quality of prescribed medicines), and a more cost-effective use of available health resources (*1, 2*).

The WHO Model List of Essential Medicines

Most countries require that a pharmaceutical product be approved on the basis of efficacy, safety and quality before it can be prescribed. The majority of health care and insurance schemes will only cover the cost of medicines on a given list. Medicines on such lists are selected after careful study of the medicines used to treat particular conditions and a comparison of the value they provide in relation to their cost. The WHO Model List of Essential Medicines (the Model List) is an example of such a list.

The first WHO Model List was drawn up in 1977 (*3*) in response to a request from the World Health Assembly (resolution WHA28.66) to the Director-General of WHO to provide Member States with advice on the selection and procurement, at reasonable costs, of essential medicines of established quality corresponding to their national health needs (*4*). The Model List has since been revised and updated 10 times (excluding the present revision) at intervals of approximately 2 years (*5–14*). Over the past two decades, the regular updating of the Model List has not only been at the heart of WHO's revised drug strategy (*15*) but has also formed a key component of the information required by Member States in relation to their medicine procurement and supply programmes.

The Model List was originally intended as a guide for the development of national and institutional essential medicine lists. It was not designed as a global standard. Nevertheless, since its introduction 25 years ago, the Model List has led to a global acceptance of the concept of essential medicines as a powerful tool for promoting health equity. By the end of 1999, 156 Member States had official essential medicines lists, of which 127 had been updated in the previous 5 years. Most countries have national lists; some have provincial or state lists as well.

The concept of essential medicines has also been adopted by many international organizations, including the United Nations Children's Fund (UNICEF) and the Office of the United Nations High Commissioner for Refugees (UNHCR), as well as nongovernmental organizations and international non-profit supply agencies. Many of these organizations base their medicine supply system on the Model List. Lists of essential medicines also guide the procurement and supply of medicines in the public sector, schemes that reimburse medicine costs, medicine donations and local medicine production, and, furthermore, are widely used as informational and educational tools by health professionals. Health insurance schemes too are increasingly using national lists of essential medicines for reference purposes.

The way in which national lists of essential medicines are developed and used has evolved over time. Initially, lists were drawn up primarily as a means to guide the procurement of medicines. More recently, however, greater emphasis has been placed on the development of treatment guidelines as the basis for medicine selection and supply, and on the evidence underlying the development of those treatment guidelines. Consequently, there has been an increasing demand for information on why a particular medicine is included in the Model List and also for references to the underlying evidence. Activities are now underway to strengthen the links between the Model List and the treatment guidelines developed by WHO.

In its present form, the Model List aims to identify cost-effective medicines for priority conditions, together with the reasons for their inclusion, linked to evidence-based clinical guidelines and with special emphasis on public health aspects and considerations of value for money. Information that supports the selection of essential medicines, such as summaries of relevant WHO clinical guidelines, systematic reviews, key references and indicative cost information is being made available via the WHO web site as the WHO Essential Medicines Library.[1] The web site provides links to other relevant sources of information, including the *WHO model formulary* and information on nomenclature and quality assurance standards. The Essential Medicines Library is under construction and will be expanded over time. Its primary function is to facilitate the work of national and institutional committees in developing national and institutional lists of essential medicines.

The current version of the Model List (the 12th) is divided into two lists, a list of "core" medicines and a list of "complementary" medicines. The core list presents a list of minimum medicine needs for a basic health care system, listing the most efficacious, safe and cost-effective medicines for priority conditions. Priority conditions are selected on the basis of current and estimated future public health relevance, and potential for safe and cost-effective treatment. The complementary list presents essential medicines for priority diseases which are efficacious, safe and cost-effective but not necessarily affordable, or for which specialized health care facilities or services may be needed.

A number of medicines in the lists are labelled with a square box symbol. This symbol indicates that a listed medicine should be seen as a representative example from a group of clinically equivalent medicines with wide experience of use, within a pharmacological class. The medicine listed on the Model List would generally be the least costly therapeutic equivalent within the group. National lists should not use a similar symbol and should be specific in their final selection, which would depend on local availability and price.

Procedures for updating the Model List
The procedures for updating the Model List are in line with the WHO recommended process for developing clinical practice guidelines (*16*). The key components are a systematic approach to collecting and reviewing evidence and a transparent development process with several rounds of external review. The procedures are intended to serve as a model for developing or updating national and institutional clinical guidelines and lists of essential medicines (see Appendix 1). Further information on the procedures for updating the Model List, including descriptions of the applications and details of the review process, is available from the WHO web site.[2]

---

[1] http://www.mednet3.who.int/mf/.
[2] http://www.who.int/medicines.

Selection criteria
The choice of essential medicines depends on several factors, including public health relevance and the availability of data on the efficacy, safety and comparative cost-effectiveness of available treatments. Factors such as stability in various conditions, the need for special diagnostic or treatment facilities and pharmacokinetic properties are also considered if appropriate. In adapting the Model List to their own needs, countries often consider factors such as local demography and the pattern of prevalent diseases; treatment facilities; training and experience of available personnel; local availability of individual pharmaceutical products; financial resources; and environmental factors.

The selection of essential medicines must be based on valid scientific evidence; only medicines for which sound and adequate data on efficacy and safety are available should be selected. In the absence of adequate scientific evidence on current treatment of a priority disease, the WHO Expert Committee on the Selection and Use of Essential Medicines may either defer its decision regarding selection until more evidence becomes available, or choose to make recommendations based on expert opinion and experience.

Most essential medicines should be formulated as single compounds. Fixed-dose combination products are selected only when the combination has a proven advantage over single compounds administered separately in therapeutic effect, safety, adherence or in delaying the development of drug resistance in malaria, tuberculosis and HIV/AIDS.

When making cost comparisons between medicines, the cost of the total treatment, not just the unit cost of the medicine, is considered. Cost and cost-effectiveness comparisons may be made among alternative treatments within the same therapeutic group, but are generally not made across therapeutic categories (e.g. between the treatment of tuberculosis and the treatment of malaria). The absolute cost of the treatment does not constitute a reason to exclude a medicine from the Model List that otherwise meets the stated selection criteria. The patent status of a medicine is not considered when selecting medicines for the Model List.

Quality assurance
Priority should be given to ensuring that available medicines have been made according to good manufacturing practices (*17*) and are of assured quality. Factors that need to be considered include:

— knowledge of, and confidence in, the origin of the product;
— the pharmaceutical stability of the product, particularly in the environment that it will be used;
— where relevant, bioavailability and bioequivalence information.

It is recommended that all medicines be purchased from known manufacturers, their duly accredited agents, or recognized international agencies known to apply high standards in selecting their suppliers.

Promoting rational use of essential medicines

The selection of essential medicines is only one step towards the improvement of the quality of health care; selection needs to be followed by appropriate use. Each individual should receive the right medicine, in an adequate dose for an adequate duration, with appropriate information and follow-up treatment, and at an affordable cost. Within different countries and settings, this is influenced by a number of factors, such as regulatory decisions, procurement, information, training, and the context in which medicines are prescribed or recommended.

Training, education and the provision of medicines information

To ensure the safe, effective and prudent use of essential medicines, access to relevant, reliable and independent information on medicines is vital. Health care professionals should receive education about the use of medicines not only during their training but also throughout their careers. The more highly trained individuals should be encouraged to assume responsibility for educating those with less training. Health care providers and pharmacists who are responsible for dispensing medicines should take every opportunity to inform consumers about the rational use of products, including those for self-medication, at the time they are dispensed.

Governments, universities and professional associations have a critical role to play with regard to the improvement of undergraduate, postgraduate and continuing education in clinical pharmacology, therapeutics and medicines information issues. Problem-based pharmacotherapy teaching has been shown to be a particularly effective strategy in this area (*18*).

Well presented and appropriate information about medicines not only ensures that they are used properly but also decreases the inappropriate use of medicines. Health ministries have a responsibility to arrange for the provision of such information. Independent medicines information activities should also be properly funded and, if necessary, financed through health care budgets. Electronic, readily accessible sources of medicines information are becoming more widely available and can form the basis of reliable medicines information systems in many settings.

Standard clinical guidelines

Standard clinical guidelines are an effective tool for assisting health professionals to choose the most appropriate medicine for a given patient with a given condition. They should be developed at national and local levels and updated on a regular basis. In order to be effective, however, standard clinical guidelines require the support of appropriate education and training programmes aimed at encouraging their use.

Drugs and therapeutic committees

Drugs and therapeutic committees can play an important role in the development and implementation of effective essential medicines programmes. Such committees should be encouraged to select products for local use from a national essential medicines list, to measure and monitor the use of these products in their own environments and to undertake interventions to improve their rational use. There is good evidence to suggest that involving both drugs and therapeutic committees and prescribers in guideline development can contribute to improved prescribing behaviour (*19*).

Measuring and monitoring medicine use

The purpose of drug utilization studies is to examine the development, regulation, marketing, distribution, prescription, dispensing and use of medicines within a society, with special emphasis on the medical, social and economic consequences. Studies of this type consider all levels of the therapeutic chain, from the development of medicines to their use by consumers. Drug utilization studies can be medicine-oriented (i.e. focused on the use of a particular medicine or group of medicines) or problem-oriented (i.e. focused on the treatment of a particular condition or disease) and can provide consumption indicators for a given country, area or institution.

Consumption can be measured in terms of economic expenditure (either in absolute terms or as a percentage of the total health budget), the number of units, or as Defined Daily Doses (DDDs) (*20*). However, it is generally recommended that utilization studies be conducted using the Anatomical Therapeutic Chemical (ATC) classification and the DDD as the measuring unit, especially when making international comparisons on the use of medicines.

The efficacy of a medicine is best assessed on the basis of randomized clinical trials, which, if well conducted, provide reliable estimates of the treatment effect of a new medicine. However, clinical trials cannot be conducted in all possible populations or settings and therefore their results must be translated into routine clinical practice with care. Given that drug utilization studies provide data on the use and the effects of medicines in routine conditions, they can provide additional evidence for the evaluation of the effectiveness of a medicine.

Drug utilization studies and clinical trials are important tools for identifying those factors or elements of the therapeutic chain in need of improvement or change. The results of such studies should be taken into consideration when taking regulatory action, selecting medicines, or designing information, training and teaching programmes.

Monitoring of medicine safety and pharmacovigilance

Safety monitoring is an important part of the overall surveillance of medicine use. The aims of the various forms of pharmacovigilance are to identify new, previously unrecognized adverse effects of medicines, to quantify their risks, and to communicate these to drug regulatory authorities, health professionals, and, when relevant, the public. Voluntary reporting of adverse effects of medicines, on which the International WHO Programme for Drug Monitoring is based, has been effective in identifying a number of previously undescribed effects. Voluntary reporting schemes, together with other methods for assembling case series, can identify certain local safety problems, and thus form the basis for specific regulatory or educational interventions. The magnitude of the risk of adverse effects is generally evaluated using observational epidemiological methods, such as case-control, cohort and case-population studies. Each country and institution should set up simple schemes aimed at identifying problems related to the safety of medicines.

The WHO Model List of Essential Medicines: core list

Explanatory notes

The core list presents a list of minimum medicine needs for a basic health care system, listing the most efficacious, safe and cost-effective medicines for priority conditions. Priority conditions are selected on the basis of current and estimated future public health relevance, and potential for safe and cost-effective treatment.

When the strength of a medicine is specified in terms of a selected salt or ester, this is mentioned in brackets; when it refers to the active moiety, the name of the salt or ester in brackets is preceded by the word "as".

Many medicines included in the Model List are preceded by a square box symbol (□) to indicate that they represent an example of a therapeutic group and that various medicines could serve as alternatives. It is imperative that this is understood when medicines are selected at national level, since choice is then influenced by the comparative cost and availability of equivalent products. Examples of acceptable substitutions include:

— hydrochlorothiazide: any other thiazide-type diuretic currently in broad clinical use;
— hydralazine: any other peripheral vasodilator having an antihypertensive effect;
— senna: any mild stimulant laxative (either synthetic or of plant origin).

Numbers in parentheses following the medicine names indicate:

(1) Medicines subject to international control under: (a) the Single Convention on Narcotic Drugs, 1961 (*21*); (b) the Convention on Psychotropic Substances, 1971 (*22*); or (c) the United Nations Convention against Illicit Traffic in Narcotic Drugs and Psychotropic Substances, 1988 (*23*).
(2) Specific expertise, diagnostic precision, individualization of dosage or special equipment required for proper use.
(3) Greater potency or efficacy.
(4) In renal insufficiency, contraindicated or dosage adjustments necessary.
(5) To improve compliance.
(6) Special pharmacokinetic properties.
(7) Adverse effects diminish benefit/risk ratio.
(8) Limited indications or narrow spectrum of activity.
(9) For epidural anaesthesia.

(10) Sustained-release preparations are available. A proposal to include such a product in a national list of essential medicines should be supported by adequate documentation.
(11) Monitoring of therapeutic concentrations in plasma can improve safety and efficacy.

Medicines are grouped according to therapeutic categories. The numbers preceding the sections and subsections have, in general, been allocated in accordance with English alphabetical order; they have no formal significance. Within sections, medicines are listed in alphabetical order.

Certain pharmacological effects have many therapeutic uses. Medicines with multiple uses could be listed under several therapeutic categories in the Model List. However, the inclusion of such medicines in more than one therapeutic category has been limited to those circumstances that the Expert Committee wishes to emphasize. Medicines in the Model List are therefore not listed in all of the therapeutic categories in which they are of value. Detailed information on the therapeutic use of essential medicines is available in the *WHO model formulary (24)*.

Medicine	Route of administration, dosage forms and strengths

1. Anaesthetics

1.1 *General anaesthetics and oxygen*

ether, anaesthetic (1c, 2)	inhalation
halothane (2)	inhalation
ketamine (2)	injection, 50 mg (as hydrochloride)/ml in 10-ml vial
nitrous oxide (2)	inhalation
oxygen	inhalation (medicinal gas)
☐ thiopental (2)	powder for injection, 0.5 g, 1.0 g (sodium salt) in ampoule

1.2 *Local anaesthetics*

☐ bupivacaine (2, 9)	injection, 0.25%, 0.5% (hydrochloride) in vial
	injection for spinal anaesthesia, 0.5% (hydrochloride) in 4-ml ampoule to be mixed with 7.5% glucose solution
☐ lidocaine	injection, 1%, 2% (hydrochloride) in vial
	injection for spinal anaesthesia, 5% (hydrochloride) in 2-ml ampoule to be mixed with 7.5% glucose solution
	topical forms, 2–4% (hydrochloride)
☐ lidocaine + epinephrine (adrenaline)	injection, 1%, 2% (hydrochloride) + epinephrine 1:200 000 in vial
	dental cartridge, 2% (hydrochloride) + epinephrine 1:80 000

1.3 *Preoperative medication and sedation for short-term procedures*

atropine	injection, 1 mg (sulfate) in 1-ml ampoule
chloral hydrate	syrup, 200 mg/5 ml
☐ diazepam (1b)	injection, 5 mg/ml in 2-ml ampoule
	tablet, 5 mg

☐ Example of a therapeutic group.

Medicine	Route of administration, dosage forms and strengths

1. Anaesthetics (continued)

1.3 Preoperative medication and sedation for short-term procedures (continued)

□ morphine (1a)	injection, 10 mg (hydrochloride or sulfate) in 1-ml ampoule
□ promethazine	elixir or syrup, 5 mg (hydrochloride)/5 ml

2. Analgesics, antipyretics, nonsteroidal anti-inflammatory medicines, medicines used to treat gout and disease-modifying agents used in rheumatoid disorders

2.1 Non-opioid analgesics and antipyretics and nonsteroidal anti-inflammatory medicines

acetylsalicylic acid	tablet, 100–500 mg
	suppository, 50–150 mg
□ ibuprofen	tablet, 200 mg, 400 mg
paracetamol	tablet, 100–500 mg
	suppository, 100 mg
	syrup, 125 mg/5 ml

2.2 Opioid analgesics

□ codeine (1a)	tablet, 30 mg (phosphate)
□ morphine (1a)	injection, 10 mg (hydrochloride or sulfate) in 1-ml ampoule
	oral solution, 10 mg (hydrochloride or sulfate)/5 ml
	tablet, 10 mg (sulfate)

2.3 Medicines used to treat gout

allopurinol (4)	tablet, 100 mg
colchicine (7)	tablet, 500 µg

2.4 Disease-modifying agents used in rheumatoid disorders

azathioprine (2)	tablet, 50 mg
chloroquine (2)	tablet, 100 mg, 150 mg (as phosphate or sulfate)
cyclophosphamide (2)	tablet, 25 mg

□ Example of a therapeutic group.

Medicine	Route of administration, dosage forms and strengths

2. Analgesics, antipyretics, nonsteroidal anti-inflammatory medicines, medicines used to treat gout and disease-modifying agents used in rheumatoid disorders (*continued*)

2.4 *Disease-modifying agents used in rheumatoid disorders* (*continued*)

methotrexate (2)	tablet, 2.5 mg (as sodium salt)
penicillamine (2)	capsule or tablet, 250 mg
sulfasalazine (2)	tablet, 500 mg

3. Antiallergics and medicines used in anaphylaxis

▫ chlorphenamine	tablet, 4 mg (hydrogen maleate)
	injection, 10 mg (hydrogen maleate) in 1-ml ampoule
▫ dexamethasone	tablet, 500 µg, 4 mg
	injection, 4 mg dexamethasone phosphate (as disodium salt) in 1-ml ampoule
epinephrine (adrenaline)	injection, 1 mg (as hydrochloride or hydrogen tartrate) in 1-ml ampoule
hydrocortisone	powder for injection, 100 mg (as sodium succinate) in vial
▫ prednisolone	tablet, 5 mg

4. Antidotes and other substances used in poisonings

4.1 *Nonspecific*

▫ charcoal, activated	powder
ipecacuanha	syrup, containing 0.14% ipecacuanha alkaloids calculated as emetine

4.2 *Specific*

acetylcysteine	injection, 200 mg/ml in 10-ml ampoule
atropine	injection, 1 mg (sulfate) in 1-ml ampoule
calcium gluconate (2, 8)	injection, 100 mg/ml in 10-ml ampoule
deferoxamine	powder for injection, 500 mg (mesilate) in vial
dimercaprol (2)	injection in oil, 50 mg/ml in 2-ml ampoule

▫ Example of a therapeutic group.

Medicine	Route of administration, dosage forms and strengths

4. Antidotes and other substances used in poisonings (*continued*)

4.2 *Specific* (*continued*)

☐ DL-methionine	tablet, 250 mg
methylthioninium chloride (methylene blue)	injection, 10 mg/ml in 10-ml ampoule
naloxone	injection, 400 µg (hydrochloride) in 1-ml ampoule
penicillamine (2)	capsule or tablet, 250 mg
potassium ferric hexacyanoferrate (II)·2H$_2$O (Prussian blue)	powder for oral administration
sodium calcium edetate (2)	injection, 200 mg/ml in 5-ml ampoule
sodium nitrite	injection, 30 mg/ml in 10-ml ampoule
sodium thiosulfate	injection, 250 mg/ml in 50-ml ampoule

5. Anticonvulsants/antiepileptics

carbamazepine (10, 11)	scored tablet, 100 mg, 200 mg
☐ diazepam (1b)	injection, 5 mg/ml in 2-ml ampoule (intravenous or rectal)
ethosuximide	capsule, 250 mg
	syrup, 250 mg/5 ml
magnesium sulfate	injection, 500 mg/ml in 2-ml ampoule, 500 mg/ml in 10-ml ampoule
phenobarbital (1b, 11)	tablet, 15–100 mg
	elixir, 15 mg/5 ml
phenytoin (7, 11)	capsule or tablet, 25 mg, 50 mg, 100 mg (sodium salt)
	injection, 50 mg (sodium salt)/ml in 5-ml vial
valproic acid (7, 11)	enteric coated tablet, 200 mg, 500 mg (sodium salt)

☐ Example of a therapeutic group.

Medicine	Route of administration, dosage forms and strengths

6. Anti-infective medicines

6.1 *Anthelminthics*

6.1.1 *Intestinal anthelminthics*

albendazole	chewable tablet, 400 mg
levamisole	tablet, 50 mg, 150 mg (as hydrochloride)
□ mebendazole	chewable tablet, 100 mg, 500 mg
niclosamide	chewable tablet, 500 mg
praziquantel	tablet, 150 mg, 600 mg
pyrantel	chewable tablet, 250 mg (as embonate)
	oral suspension, 50 mg (as embonate)/ml

6.1.2 *Antifilarials*

diethylcarbamazine	tablet, 50 mg, 100 mg (dihydrogen citrate)
ivermectin	scored tablet, 3 mg, 6 mg

6.1.3 *Antischistosomals and other antitrematode medicines*

praziquantel	tablet, 600 mg
triclabendazole	tablet, 250 mg

6.2 *Antibacterials*

6.2.1 *β-Lactam medicines*

□ amoxicillin	capsule or tablet, 250 mg, 500 mg (anhydrous)
	powder for oral suspension, 125 mg (anhydrous)/5 ml
ampicillin	powder for injection, 500 mg, 1 g (as sodium salt) in vial
benzathine benzylpenicillin	powder for injection, 1.44 g benzylpenicillin (= 2.4 million IU) in 5-ml vial
benzylpenicillin	powder for injection, 600 mg (= 1 million IU), 3 g (= 5 million IU) (sodium or potassium salt) in vial

---

□ Example of a therapeutic group.

Medicine	Route of administration, dosage forms and strengths

6. Anti-infective medicines (*continued*)

6.2 *Antibacterials* (*continued*)

6.2.1 *β-Lactam medicines* (*continued*)

☐ cloxacillin

capsule, 500 mg, 1 g (as sodium salt)

powder for oral solution, 125 mg (as sodium salt)/5 ml

powder for injection, 500 mg (as sodium salt) in vial

phenoxymethylpenicillin

tablet, 250 mg (as potassium salt)

powder for oral suspension, 250 mg (as potassium salt)/5 ml

procaine benzylpenicillin

powder for injection, 1 g (= 1 million IU), 3 g (= 3 million IU) in vial

6.2.2 *Other antibacterials*

☐ chloramphenicol (7)

capsule, 250 mg

oral suspension, 150 mg (as palmitate)/5 ml

powder for injection, 1 g (as sodium succinate) in vial

☐ ciprofloxacin

tablet, 250 mg (as hydrochloride)

☐ doxycycline (5, 6)

capsule or tablet, 100 mg (hydrochloride)

☐ erythromycin

capsule or tablet, 250 mg (as stearate or ethyl succinate)

powder for oral suspension, 125 mg (as stearate or ethyl succinate)

powder for injection, 500 mg (as lactobionate) in vial

☐ gentamicin (2, 4, 7, 11)

injection, 10 mg, 40 mg (as sulfate)/ml in 2-ml vial

☐ metronidazole

tablet, 200–500 mg

injection, 500 mg in 100-ml vial

suppository, 500 mg, 1 g

oral suspension, 200 mg (as benzoate)/5 ml

nalidixic acid (8)

tablet, 250 mg, 500 mg

☐ Example of a therapeutic group.

Medicine	Route of administration, dosage forms and strengths

6. Anti-infective medicines (*continued*)

6.2 *Antibacterials* (*continued*)

6.2.2 *Other antibacterials* (*continued*)

nitrofurantoin (4, 8)	tablet, 100 mg
spectinomycin (8)	powder for injection, 2 g (as hydrochloride) in vial
□ sulfadiazine (4)	tablet, 500 mg
	injection, 250 mg (sodium salt) in 4-ml ampoule
□ sulfamethoxazole + trimethoprim (4)	tablet, 100 mg + 20 mg, 400 mg + 80 mg
	oral suspension, 200 mg + 40 mg/5 ml
	injection, 80 mg + 16 mg/ml in 5-ml ampoule, 80 mg + 16 mg/ml in 10-ml ampoule
trimethoprim (8)	tablet, 100 mg, 200 mg
	injection, 20 mg/ml in 5-ml ampoule

6.2.3 *Antileprosy medicines*

clofazimine	capsule, 50 mg, 100 mg
dapsone	tablet, 25 mg, 50 mg, 100 mg
rifampicin	capsule or tablet, 150 mg, 300 mg

6.2.4 *Antituberculosis medicines*

ethambutol (4)	tablet, 100–400 mg (hydrochloride)
isoniazid	tablet, 100–300 mg
isoniazid + ethambutol (5)	tablet, 150 mg + 400 mg
pyrazinamide	tablet, 400 mg
rifampicin	capsule or tablet, 150 mg, 300 mg
rifampicin + isoniazid (5)	tablet, 60 mg + 30 mg, 150 mg + 75 mg, 300 mg + 150 mg, 60 mg + 60 mg[a], 150 mg + 150 mg[a]
rifampicin + isoniazid + pyrazinamide (5)	tablet, 60 mg + 30 mg + 150 mg, 150 mg + 75 mg + 400 mg, 150 mg + 150 mg + 500 mg[a]

[a] For intermittent use three times weekly.
□ Example of a therapeutic group.

6. Anti-infective medicines (*continued*)

6.2 Antibacterials (*continued*)

6.2.4 *Antituberculosis medicines* (*continued*)

rifampicin + isoniazid + pyrazinamide + ethambutol	tablet, 150 mg + 75 mg + 400 mg + 275 mg
streptomycin (4)	powder for injection, 1 g (as sulfate) in vial

6.3 Antifungal medicines

amphotericin B (4)	powder for injection, 50 mg in vial
☐ fluconazole	capsule, 50 mg
	injection, 2 mg/ml in vial
	oral suspension, 50 mg/5 ml
griseofulvin (7)	capsule or tablet, 125 mg, 250 mg
nystatin	tablet, 100 000 IU, 500 000 IU
	lozenge, 100 000 IU
	pessary, 100 000 IU

6.4 Antiviral medicines

6.4.1 *Antiherpes medicines*

aciclovir (8)	tablet, 200 mg
	powder for injection, 250 mg (as sodium salt) in vial

6.4.2 *Antiretroviral medicines*

The antiretroviral medicines do not cure the HIV infection, they only temporarily suppress viral replication and improve symptoms. They have various adverse effects and patients receiving these medicines require careful monitoring by adequately trained health professionals. For these reasons, continued rigorous promotion of measures to prevent new infections is essential and the need for this has not been diminished in any way by the addition of antiretroviral medicines to the Model List. Adequate resources and trained health professionals are a prerequisite for the introduction of this class of medicines. Effective therapy requires commencement of three or four medicines simultaneously, and alternative regimens are necessary to meet specific requirements at start-up, to substitute for first-line regimens in the case of toxicity, or to replace failing regimens. The Committee strongly recommends the use of three- or four-medicine combinations as specifically recommended in the

☐ Example of a therapeutic group.

Medicine	Route of administration, dosage forms and strengths

6. Anti-infective medicines (*continued*)

6.4 *Antiviral medicines* (*continued*)

6.4.2 *Antiretroviral medicines* (*continued*)

WHO treatment guidelines (*25*). The use of fixed-dose preparations for these combinations is also recommended, with assured pharmaceutical quality and interchangeability with the single products as approved by the relevant drug regulatory authority.

(a) Nucleoside reverse transcriptase inhibitors

abacavir (ABC)	tablet, 300 mg (as sulfate)
	oral solution, 100 mg (as sulfate)/5 ml
didanosine (ddI)	buffered chewable dispersible tablet, 25 mg, 50 mg, 100 mg, 150 mg, 200 mg
	buffered powder for oral solution, 100 mg, 167 mg, 250 mg packet
	unbuffered enteric coated capsule, 125 mg, 200 mg, 250 mg, 400 mg
lamivudine (3TC)	tablet, 150 mg
	oral solution, 50 mg/5 ml
stavudine (d4T)	capsule, 15 mg, 20 mg, 30 mg, 40 mg
	powder for oral solution, 5 mg/5 ml
zidovudine (ZDV or AZT)	tablet, 300 mg
	capsule, 100 mg, 250 mg
	oral solution or syrup, 50 mg/5 ml
	solution for IV infusion injection, 10 mg/ml in 20-ml vial

(b) Non-nucleoside reverse transcriptase inhibitors

efavirenz (EFV or EFZ)	capsule, 50 mg, 100 mg, 200 mg
	oral solution, 150 mg/5 ml
nevirapine (NVP)	tablet, 200 mg
	oral suspension, 50 mg/5 ml

(c) Protease inhibitors

Selection of two or three protease inhibitors from the Model List will need to be determined by each country after consideration of local clinical guidelines

---

□ Example of a therapeutic group.

Medicine	Route of administration, dosage forms and strengths

6. Anti-infective medicines (continued)

6.4 Antiviral medicines (continued)

6.4.2 Antiretroviral medicines (continued)

(c) Protease inhibitors (continued)

and experience, as well as the comparative costs of available products. Ritonavir is recommended for use in combination with indinavir, lopinavir and saquinavir as a booster, and not as a medicine in its own right.

indinavir (IDV)	capsule, 200 mg, 333 mg, 400 mg (as sulfate)
lopinavir + ritonavir (LPV/r)	capsule, 133.3 mg + 33.3 mg oral solution, 400 mg + 100 mg/5 ml
nelfinavir (NFV)	tablet, 250 mg (as mesilate)
	oral powder, 50 mg/g
ritonavir(r)	capsule, 100 mg
	oral solution, 400 mg/5 ml
saquinavir (SQV)	capsule, 200 mg

6.5 Antiprotozoal medicines

6.5.1 Antiamoebic and antigiardiasis medicines

☐ diloxanide	tablet, 500 mg (furoate)
☐ metronidazole	tablet, 200–500 mg
	injection, 500 mg in 100-ml vial
	oral suspension, 200 mg (as benzoate)/5 ml

6.5.2 Antileishmaniasis medicines

☐ meglumine antimoniate	injection, 30%, equivalent to approximately 8.1% antimony, in 5-ml ampoule
pentamidine (5)	powder for injection, 200 mg, 300 mg (isetionate) in vial

6.5.3 Antimalarial medicines

(a) For curative treatment

artemether + lumefantrine[a]	tablet, 20 mg + 120 mg

---

[a] Recommended for use in areas with significant drug resistance and not in pregnancy or in children below 10 kg.

☐ Example of a therapeutic group.

Medicine	Route of administration, dosage forms and strengths

6. Anti-infective medicines (*continued*)

6.5 *Antiprotozoal medicines* (*continued*)

6.5.3 *Antimalarial medicines* (*continued*)

(a) For curative treatment (*continued*)

☐ chloroquine	tablet, 100 mg, 150 mg (as phosphate or sulfate)
	syrup, 50 mg (as phosphate or sulfate)/5 ml
	injection, 40 mg (as hydrochloride, phosphate or sulfate)/ml in 5-ml ampoule
primaquine	tablet, 7.5 mg, 15 mg (as diphosphate)
☐ quinine	tablet, 300 mg (as bisulfate or sulfate)
	injection, 300 mg (dihydrochloride)/ml in 2-ml ampoule

(b) For prophylaxis

chloroquine	tablet, 150 mg (as phosphate or sulfate)
	syrup, 50 mg (as phosphate or sulfate)/5 ml
doxycycline	capsule or tablet, 100 mg (hydrochloride)
mefloquine	tablet, 250 mg (as hydrochloride)
proguanil[a]	tablet, 100 mg (hydrochloride)

6.5.4 *Antipneumocystosis and antitoxoplasmosis medicines*

pentamidine (2)	tablet, 200 mg, 300 mg
pyrimethamine	tablet, 25 mg
sulfamethoxazole + trimethoprim	injection, 80 mg + 16 mg/ml in 5-ml ampoule, 80 mg + 16 mg/ml in 10-ml ampoule

6.5.5 *Antitrypanosomal medicines*

(a) African trypanosomiasis

melarsoprol (2)	injection, 3.6% solution
pentamidine (2)	powder for injection, 200 mg, 300 mg (isetionate) in vial
suramin sodium	powder for injection, 1 g in vial

---

[a] For use only in combination with chloroquine.
☐ Example of a therapeutic group.

Medicine	Route of administration, dosage forms and strengths

6. Anti-infective medicines (*continued*)

6.5 *Antiprotozoal medicines* (*continued*)

6.5.5 *Antitrypanosomal medicines* (*continued*)

(b) American trypanosomiasis

benznidazole (7)	tablet, 100 mg
nifurtimox (2, 8)	tablet, 30 mg, 120 mg, 250 mg

6.6 *Insect repellents*

diethyltoluamide	topical solution, 50%, 75%

7. Antimigraine medicines

7.1 *For treatment of acute attack*

acetylsalicylic acid	tablet, 300–500 mg
ergotamine (7)	tablet, 1 mg (tartrate)
paracetamol	tablet, 300–500 mg

7.2 *For prophylaxis*

☐ propranolol	tablet, 20 mg, 40 mg (hydrochloride)

8. Antineoplastics, immunosuppressives and medicines used in palliative care

8.1 *Immunosuppressive medicines* (please see complementary list)

8.2 *Cytotoxic medicines* (please see complementary list)

8.3 *Hormones and antihormones* (please see complementary list)

8.4 *Medicines used in palliative care*

The Committee recommended that all the medicines mentioned in the WHO publication, *Cancer pain relief: with a guide to opioid availability*, 2nd ed. (*26*), be considered essential. These medicines are included in the relevant sections of the Model List, according to their therapeutic use, e.g. as analgesics.

9. Antiparkinsonism medicines

☐ biperiden	tablet, 2 mg (hydrochloride)
	injection, 5 mg (lactate) in 1-ml ampoule
levodopa + ☐ carbidopa (5, 6)	tablet, 100 mg + 10 mg, 250 mg + 25 mg

---

☐ Example of a therapeutic group.

Medicine	Route of administration, dosage forms and strengths

10. Medicines affecting the blood

10.1 *Antianaemia medicines*

ferrous salt	tablet, equivalent to 60 mg iron
	oral solution, equivalent to 25 mg iron (as sulfate)/ml
ferrous salt + folic acid[a]	tablet, equivalent to 60 mg iron + 400 µg folic acid
folic acid (2)	tablet, 1 mg, 5 mg
	injection, 1 mg (as sodium salt) in 1-ml ampoule
hydroxocobalamin (2)	injection, 1 mg in 1-ml ampoule

10.2 *Medicines affecting coagulation*

desmopressin (8)	injection, 4 µg (acetate)/ml in 1-ml ampoule
	nasal spray, 10 µg (acetate)/metered dose
heparin sodium	injection, 1000 IU/ml, 5000 IU/ml, 20 000 IU/ml in 1-ml ampoule
phytomenadione	injection, 10 mg/ml in 5-ml ampoule
	tablet, 10 mg
protamine sulfate	injection, 10 mg/ml in 5-ml ampoule
☐ warfarin (2, 6)	tablet, 1 mg, 2 mg, 5 mg (sodium salt)

11. Blood products and plasma substitutes

11.1 *Plasma substitutes*

☐ dextran 70	injectable solution, 6%
☐ polygeline	injectable solution, 3.5%

11.2 *Plasma fractions for specific uses* (please see complementary list)

12. Cardiovascular medicines

12.1 *Antianginal medicines*

☐ atenolol	tablet, 50 mg, 100 mg
glyceryl trinitrate	tablet (sublingual), 500 µg

---

[a] Nutritional supplement for use during pregnancy.
☐ Example of a therapeutic group.

Medicine	Route of administration, dosage forms and strengths

12. Cardiovascular medicines (*continued*)

12.1 *Antianginal medicines* (*continued*)

☐ isosorbide dinitrate — tablet (sublingual), 5 mg

☐ verapamil (10) — tablet, 40 mg, 80 mg (hydrochloride)

12.2 *Antiarrhythmic medicines*

☐ atenolol — tablet, 50 mg, 100 mg

digoxin (4, 11) — tablet, 62.5 µg, 250 µg

oral solution, 50 µg/ml

injection, 250 µg/ml in 2-ml ampoule

lidocaine — injection, 20 mg (hydrochloride)/ml in 5-ml ampoule

verapamil (8, 10) — tablet, 40 mg, 80 mg (hydrochloride)

injection, 2.5 mg (hydrochloride)/ml in 2-ml ampoule

12.3 *Antihypertensive medicines*

☐ atenolol — tablet, 50 mg, 100 mg

☐ captopril — scored tablet, 25 mg

☐ hydralazine — tablet, 25 mg, 50 mg (hydrochloride)

powder for injection, 20 mg (hydrochloride) in ampoule

☐ hydrochlorothiazide — scored tablet, 25 mg

methyldopa (7) — tablet, 250 mg

☐ nifedipine (10) — sustained-release formulations

tablet, 10 mg

☐ reserpine — tablet, 100 µg, 250 µg

injection, 1 mg in 1-ml ampoule

12.4 *Medicines used in heart failure*

☐ captopril — scored tablet, 25 mg

digoxin (4, 11) — tablet, 62.5 µg, 250 µg

oral solution, 50 µg/ml

injection, 250 µg/ml in 2-ml ampoule

☐ Example of a therapeutic group.

Medicine	Route of administration, dosage forms and strengths

12. Cardiovascular medicines (continued)

12.4 Medicines used in heart failure (continued)

dopamine	injection, 40 mg (hydrochloride)/ml in 5-ml vial
☐ hydrochlorothiazide	tablet, 25 mg, 50 mg

12.5 Antithrombotic medicines

acetylsalicylic acid	tablet, 100 mg

12.6 Lipid-lowering agents

The Committee recognizes the value of lipid-lowering medicines in treating patients with hyperlipidaemia. β-Hydroxy-β-methylglutaryl-coenzyme A (HMG-CoA) reductase inhibitors, often referred to as "statins", are a family of potent and effective lipid-lowering medicines with a good tolerability profile. Several of these medicines have been shown to reduce the incidence of fatal and non-fatal myocardial infarction, stroke and mortality (all causes), as well as the need for coronary by-pass surgery. All remain very costly but may be cost-effective for secondary prevention of cardiovascular disease as well as for primary prevention in some very high-risk patients. Since no single medicine has been shown to be significantly more effective or less expensive than others in the group, none is included in the Model List; the choice of medicine for use in patients at highest risk should be decided at the national level.

13. Dermatological medicines (topical)

13.1 Antifungal medicines

benzoic acid + salicylic acid	ointment or cream, 6% + 3%
☐ miconazole	ointment or cream, 2% (nitrate)
sodium thiosulfate	solution, 15%

13.2 Anti-infective medicines

☐ methylrosanilinium chloride (gentian violet)	aqueous solution, 0.5%
	tincture, 0.5%
neomycin + ☐ bacitracin (7)	ointment, 5 mg neomycin sulfate + 500 IU bacitracin zinc/g
potassium permanganate	aqueous solution, 1 : 10 000
silver sulfadiazine	cream, 1%, in 500-g container

☐ Example of a therapeutic group.

Medicine	Route of administration, dosage forms and strengths

13. Dermatological medicines (topical) (*continued*)

13.3 *Anti-inflammatory and antipruritic medicines*

☐ betamethasone (3) — ointment or cream, 0.1% (as valerate)

☐ calamine lotion — lotion

☐ hydrocortisone — ointment or cream, 1% (acetate)

13.4 *Astringent medicines*

aluminium diacetate — solution, 13% for dilution

13.5 *Medicines affecting skin differentiation and proliferation*

benzoyl peroxide — lotion or cream, 5%

coal tar — solution, 5%

dithranol — ointment, 0.1–2%

fluorouracil — ointment, 5%

☐ podophyllum resin (7) — solution, 10–25%

salicylic acid — solution, 5%

urea — ointment or cream, 10%

13.6 *Scabicides and pediculicides*

☐ benzyl benzoate — lotion, 25%

permethrin — cream, 5%

— lotion, 1%

13.7 *Ultraviolet-blocking agents* (please see complementary list)

14. Diagnostic agents

14.1 *Ophthalmic medicines*

fluorescein — eye drops, 1% (sodium salt)

☐ tropicamide — eye drops, 0.5%

14.2 *Radiocontrast media*

☐ amidotrizoate — injection, 140–420 mg iodine (as sodium or meglumine salt)/ml in 20-ml ampoule

barium sulfate — aqueous suspension

☐ iohexol — injection, 140–350 mg iodine/ml in 5-ml, 10-ml or 20-ml ampoule

---

☐ Example of a therapeutic group.

Medicine	Route of administration, dosage forms and strengths

14. Diagnostic agents (*continued*)

14.2 *Radiocontrast media* (*continued*)

☐ iopanoic acid — tablet, 500 mg

☐ propyliodone — oily suspension, 500–600 mg/ml in 20-ml ampoule[a]

15. Disinfectants and antiseptics

15.1 *Antiseptics*

☐ chlorhexidine — solution, 5% (digluconate) for dilution

☐ ethanol — solution, 70% (denatured)

☐ polyvidone iodine — solution, 10%

15.2 *Disinfectants*

☐ chlorine base compound — powder (0.1% available chlorine) for solution

☐ chloroxylenol — solution, 4.8%

glutaral — solution, 2%

16. Diuretics

☐ amiloride (4, 7, 8) — tablet, 5 mg (hydrochloride)

☐ furosemide — tablet, 40 mg

injection, 10 mg/ml in 2-ml ampoule

☐ hydrochlorothiazide — tablet, 25 mg, 50 mg

spironolactone (8) — tablet, 25 mg

17. Gastrointestinal medicines

17.1 *Antacids and other antiulcer medicines*

aluminium hydroxide — tablet, 500 mg

oral suspension, 320 mg/5 ml

☐ cimetidine — tablet, 200 mg

injection, 100 mg/ml in 2-ml ampoule

magnesium hydroxide — oral suspension, equivalent to 550 mg magnesium oxide/10 ml

---

[a] For administration only into the bronchial tree.

☐ Example of a therapeutic group.

Medicine	Route of administration, dosage forms and strengths

17. Gastrointestinal medicines (*continued*)

17.2 *Antiemetic medicines*

metoclopramide	tablet, 10 mg (hydrochloride)
	injection, 5 mg (hydrochloride)/ml in 2-ml ampoule
☐ promethazine	tablet, 10 mg, 25 mg (hydrochloride)
	elixir or syrup, 5 mg (hydrochloride)/5 ml
	injection, 25 mg (hydrochloride)/ml in 2-ml ampoule

17.3 *Antihaemorrhoidal medicines*

☐ local anaesthetic, astringent and anti-inflammatory medicine	ointment or suppository

17.4 *Anti-inflammatory medicines*

☐ hydrocortisone[a]	suppository, 25 mg (acetate)
	retention enema
☐ sulfasalazine (2)	tablet, 500 mg
	suppository, 500 mg
	retention enema

17.5 *Antispasmodic medicines*

☐ atropine	tablet, 1 mg (sulfate)
	injection, 1 mg (sulfate) in 1-ml ampoule

17.6 *Laxatives*

☐ senna	tablet, 7.5 mg (sennosides) (or traditional dosage forms)

17.7 *Medicines used in diarrhoea*

17.7.1 *Oral hydration*

oral rehydration salts (for glucose–electrolyte solution)	powder, 27.9 g/l

---

[a] The square box symbol (☐) applies only to hydrocortisone, retention enema.
☐ Example of a therapeutic group.

Medicine	Route of administration, dosage forms and strengths

17. Gastrointestinal medicines (continued)

17.7 Medicines used in diarrhoea (continued)

17.7.1 Oral hydration (continued)

	Components (for 1 litre of glucose–electrolyte solution):	
	sodium chloride	3.5 g/l
	trisodium citrate dihydrate[a]	2.9 g/l
	potassium chloride	1.5 g/l
	glucose	20.0 g/l

17.7.2 Antidiarrhoeal (symptomatic) medicines

☐ codeine (1a)   tablet, 30 mg (phosphate)

18. Hormones, other endocrine medicines and contraceptives

18.1 Adrenal hormones and synthetic substitutes

☐ dexamethasone   tablet, 500 µg, 4 mg

injection, 4 mg dexamethasone phosphate (as disodium salt) in 1-ml ampoule

hydrocortisone   powder for injection, 100 mg (as sodium succinate) in vial

☐ prednisolone   tablet, 1 mg, 5 mg

18.2 Androgens (please see complementary list)

18.3 Contraceptives

18.3.1 Hormonal contraceptives

☐ ethinylestradiol +
  ☐ levonorgestrel

tablet, 30 µg + 150 µg

tablet, 50 µg + 250 µg (pack of four)

☐ ethinylestradiol +
  ☐ norethisterone

tablet, 35 µg + 1.0 mg

levonorgestrel   tablet, 0.75 mg (pack of two)

18.3.2 Intrauterine devices

copper-containing device

---

[a] Trisodium citrate dihydrate may be replaced by sodium hydrogen carbonate (sodium bicarbonate) 2.5 g/l. However, as the stability of this latter formulation is very poor under tropical conditions, it is only recommended when manufactured for immediate use.

☐ Example of a therapeutic group.

18. Hormones, other endocrine medicines and contraceptives (*continued*)

18.3 *Contraceptives* (*continued*)

18.3.3 *Barrier methods*

condoms with or without
   spermicide (nonoxinol)

diaphragms with spermicide
   (nonoxinol)

18.4 *Estrogens*

□ ethinylestradiol   tablet, 10 µg, 50 µg

18.5 *Insulins and other antidiabetic agents*

□ glibenclamide   tablet, 2.5 mg, 5 mg

insulin injection (soluble)   injection, 40 IU/ml in 10-ml vial, 100 IU/ml in 10-ml vial

intermediate-acting insulin   injection, 40 IU/ml in 10-ml vial, 100 IU/ml in 10-ml vial (as compound insulin zinc suspension or isophane insulin)

metformin   tablet, 500 mg (hydrochloride)

18.6 *Ovulation inducers*

□ clomifene (2, 8)   tablet, 50 mg (citrate)

18.7 *Progestogens*

norethisterone   tablet, 5 mg

18.8 *Thyroid hormones and antithyroid medicines*

levothyroxine   tablet, 50 µg, 100 µg (sodium salt)

potassium iodide   tablet, 60 mg

□ propylthiouracil   tablet, 50 mg

19. Immunologicals

19.1 *Diagnostic agents*

All tuberculins should comply with the Requirements for Tuberculins (Revised 1985), as published in the thirty-sixth report of the WHO Expert Committee on Biological Standardization (*27*).

tuberculin, purified protein
   derivative (PPD)   injection

□ Example of a therapeutic group.

19. Immunologicals (continued)

19.2 Sera and immunoglobulins

All plasma fractions should comply with the Requirements for the Collection, Processing and Quality Control of Blood, Blood Components and Plasma Derivatives (Revised 1992), as published in the forty-third report of the WHO Expert Committee on Biological Standardization (28).

anti-D immunoglobulin (human)	injection, 250 µg in single-dose vial
⬚ antitetanus immunoglobulin (human)	injection, 500 IU in vial
antivenom sera	injection
diphtheria antitoxin	injection, 10 000 IU, 20 000 IU in vial
immunoglobulin, human normal (2)	injection (intramuscular)
immunoglobulin, human normal (2, 8)	injection (intravenous)
⬚ rabies immunoglobulin	injection, 150 IU/ml in vial

19.3 Vaccines

All vaccines should comply with the following requirements for biological substances, as published in the reports of the WHO Expert Committee on Biological Standardization. BCG vaccines should comply with the Requirements for Dried BCG Vaccine (Revised 1985), as published in the thirty-sixth report of the WHO Expert Committee on Biological Standardization (29) and subsequent Amendment 1987 as published in the thirty-eighth report of the WHO Expert Committee on Biological Standardization (30). Diphtheria, pertussis and tetanus vaccines should comply with the Requirements for Diphtheria, Tetanus, Pertussis and Combined Vaccines (Revised 1989), as published in the fortieth report of the WHO Expert Committee on Biological Standardization (31). Hepatitis B vaccines should comply with the Requirements for Hepatitis B Vaccine Prepared from Plasma (Revised 1994), as published in the forty-fifth report of the WHO Expert Committee on Biological Standardization (32). Measles, mumps and rubella vaccines should comply with the Requirements for Measles, Mumps and Rubella Vaccines and Combined Vaccine (Live) (Revised 1992), as published in the forty-third report of the WHO Expert Committee on Biological Standardization (33) and subsequent Note, as published in the forty-fourth report of the WHO Expert Committee on Biological Standardization (34). Poliomyelitis vaccines should comply with the Requirements for Poliomyelitis Vaccine (Oral) (Revised 1989), as published in the fortieth report of the WHO Expert Committee on Biological Standardization (35) or the Requirements for

---

⬚ Example of a therapeutic group.

19. Immunologicals (*continued*)

19.3 *Vaccines* (*continued*)

Poliomyelitis Vaccine (Inactivated) (Revised 1981), as published in the report of the WHO Expert Committee on Biological Standardization (*36*) and subsequent Addendum 1985, as published in the thirty-sixth report of the WHO Expert Committee on Biological Standardization (*37*). Influenza vaccines should comply with the Requirements for Influenza Vaccine (Inactivated) (Revised 1990), as published in the forty-first report of the WHO Expert Committee on Biological Standardization (*38*). Meningococcal meningitis vaccines should comply with the Requirements for Meningococcal Polysaccharide Vaccine, as published in the report of the WHO Expert Committee on Biological Standardization (*39*) and subsequent Addendum 1980, incorporating Addendum 1976 and Addendum 1977, as published in the thirty-first report of the WHO Expert Committee on Biological Standardization (*40*). Rabies vaccines should comply with the Requirements for Rabies Vaccine for Human Use (Revised 1980), as published in the thirty-first report of the WHO Expert Committee on Biological Standardization (*41*) and subsequent Amendment 1992, as published in the forty-third report of the WHO Expert Committee on Biological Standardization (*42*) or the Requirements for Rabies Vaccine (Inactivated) for Human Use Produced in Continuous Cell Lines (Revised 1986), as published in the thirty-seventh report of the WHO Expert Committee on Biological Standardization (*43*) and subsequent Amendment 1992, as published in the forty-third report of the WHO Expert Committee on Biological Standardization (*44*). Typhoid vaccines should comply with the Requirements for Typhoid Vaccine (Live, Attenuated, Ty 21a, Oral), as published in the report of the WHO Expert Committee on Biological Standardization (*45*) or the Requirements for Vi Polysaccharide Typhoid Vaccine, as published in the forty-third report of the WHO Expert Committee on Biological Standardization (*46*). Yellow fever vaccines should comply with Requirements for Yellow Fever Vaccine (Revised 1995), as published in the forty-sixth report of the WHO Expert Committee on Biological Standardization (*47*).

19.3.1 *For universal immunization*

BCG vaccine

diphtheria vaccine

hepatitis B vaccine

measles vaccine

pertussis vaccine

poliomyelitis vaccine

tetanus vaccine

□ Example of a therapeutic group.

19. Immunologicals (*continued*)

19.3 Vaccines (*continued*)

19.3.2 *For specific groups of individuals*

influenza vaccine

meningococcal meningitis vaccine

mumps vaccine

rabies vaccine (inactivated)
   (prepared in cell culture)

rubella vaccine

typhoid vaccine

yellow fever vaccine

20. Muscle relaxants (peripherally-acting) and cholinesterase inhibitors

☐ alcuronium (2) — injection, 5 mg (chloride)/ml in 2-ml ampoule

☐ neostigmine — tablet, 15 mg (bromide)

injection, 500 µg, 2.5 mg (metilsulfate) in 1-ml ampoule

pyridostigmine (2, 8) — tablet, 60 mg (bromide)

injection, 1 mg in 1-ml ampoule

suxamethonium (2) — injection, 50 mg (chloride)/ml in 2-ml ampoule

powder for injection (chloride), in vial

21. Ophthalmological preparations

21.1 Anti-infective agents

☐ gentamicin — solution (eye drops), 0.3% (as sulfate)

☐ idoxuridine — solution (eye drops), 0.1%

eye ointment, 0.2%

silver nitrate — solution (eye drops), 1%

☐ tetracycline — eye ointment, 1% (hydrochloride)

☐ Example of a therapeutic group.

Medicine	Route of administration, dosage forms and strengths

21. Ophthalmological preparations (*continued*)

21.2 *Anti-inflammatory agents*

☐ prednisolone — solution (eye drops), 0.5% (sodium phosphate)

21.3 *Local anaesthetics*

☐ tetracaine — solution (eye drops), 0.5% (hydrochloride)

21.4 *Miotics and antiglaucoma medicines*

acetazolamide — tablet, 250 mg

☐ pilocarpine — solution (eye drops), 2%, 4% (hydrochloride or nitrate)

☐ timolol — solution (eye drops), 0.25%, 0.5% (as maleate)

21.5 *Mydriatics*

atropine — solution (eye drops), 0.1%, 0.5%, 1% (sulfate)

22. Oxytocics and antioxytocics

22.1 *Oxytocics*

☐ ergometrine — tablet, 200 µg (hydrogen maleate)

injection, 200 µg (hydrogen maleate) in 1-ml ampoule

oxytocin — injection, 10 IU in 1-ml ampoule

22.2 *Antioxytocics*

☐ salbutamol (2) — tablet, 4 mg (as sulfate)

injection, 50 µg (as sulfate)/ml in 5-ml ampoule

23. Peritoneal dialysis solution

intraperitoneal dialysis solution (of appropriate composition) — parenteral solution

---

☐ Example of a therapeutic group.

Medicine	Route of administration, dosage forms and strengths

24. Psychotherapeutic medicines

24.1 *Medicines used in psychotic disorders*

☐ chlorpromazine

tablet, 100 mg (hydrochloride)

syrup, 25 mg (hydrochloride)/5 ml

injection, 25 mg (hydrochloride)/ml in 2-ml ampoule

☐ fluphenazine (5)

injection, 25 mg (decanoate or enantate) in 1-ml ampoule

☐ haloperidol

tablet, 2 mg, 5 mg

injection, 5 mg in 1-ml ampoule

24.2 *Medicines used in mood disorders*

24.2.1 *Medicines used in depressive disorders*

☐ amitriptyline

tablet, 25 mg (hydrochloride)

24.2.2 *Medicines used in bipolar disorders*

carbamazepine (10, 11)

scored tablet, 100 mg, 200 mg

lithium carbonate (2, 4)

capsule or tablet, 300 mg

valproic acid (7, 11)

enteric coated tablet, 200 mg, 500 mg (sodium salt)

24.3 *Medicines used in generalized anxiety and sleep disorders*

☐ diazepam (1b)

scored tablet, 2 mg, 5 mg

24.4 *Medicines used in obsessive–compulsive disorders and panic attacks*

clomipramine

capsule, 10 mg, 25 mg (hydrochloride)

25. Medicines acting on the respiratory tract

25.1 *Antiasthmatic medicines*

☐ aminophylline (2)

injection, 25 mg/ml in 10-ml ampoule

☐ beclometasone

inhalation (aerosol), 50 μg, 250 μg (dipropionate) per dose

☐ epinephrine (adrenaline)

injection, 1 mg (as hydrochloride or hydrogen tartrate) in 1-ml ampoule

---

☐ Example of a therapeutic group.

Medicine	Route of administration, dosage forms and strengths

25. Medicines acting on the respiratory tract (continued)

25.1 Antiasthmatic medicines (continued)

ipratropium bromide	inhalation (aerosol), 20 µg/metered dose
□ salbutamol	tablet, 2 mg, 4 mg (as sulfate)
	inhalation (aerosol), 100 µg (as sulfate) per dose
	syrup, 2 mg (as sulfate)/5 ml
	injection, 50 µg (as sulfate)/ml in 5-ml ampoule
	respirator solution for use in nebulizers, 5 mg (as sulfate)/ml
theophylline (10, 11)	tablet, 100 mg, 200 mg, 300 mg

25.2 Antitussive medicines

□ dextromethorphan	oral solution, 3.5 mg (bromide)/5 ml

26. Solutions correcting water, electrolyte and acid–base disturbances

26.1 Oral

oral rehydration salts (for glucose–electrolyte solution)	For composition see section 17.7.1
potassium chloride	powder for solution

26.2 Parenteral

glucose	injectable solution, 5%, 10% isotonic, 50% hypertonic
glucose with sodium chloride	injectable solution, 4% glucose, 0.18% sodium chloride (equivalent to Na^+ 30 mmol/l, Cl^- 30 mmol/l)
potassium chloride (2)	11.2% solution in 20-ml ampoule (equivalent to K^+ 1.5 mmol/ml, Cl^- 1.5 mmol/ml)
sodium chloride	injectable solution, 0.9% isotonic (equivalent to Na^+ 154 mmol/l, Cl^- 154 mmol/l

---

□ Example of a therapeutic group.

Medicine	Route of administration, dosage forms and strengths

26. Solutions correcting water, electrolyte and acid–base disturbances (*continued*)

26.2 *Parenteral* (*continued*)

sodium hydrogen carbonate	injectable solution, 1.4% isotonic (equivalent to Na^+ 167 mmol/l, HCO_3^- 167 mmol/l), 8.4% solution in 10-ml ampoule (equivalent to Na^+ 1000 mmol/l, HCO_3^- 1000 mmol/l)
☐ compound solution of sodium lactate	injectable solution

26.3 *Miscellaneous*

water for injection	2-ml, 5-ml, 10-ml ampoules

27. Vitamins and minerals

ascorbic acid	tablet, 50 mg
☐ ergocalciferol	capsule or tablet, 1.25 mg (50 000 IU)
	oral solution, 250 µg/ml (10 000 IU/ml)
iodine (8)	iodized oil, 1 ml (480 mg iodine), 0.5 ml (240 mg iodine) in ampoule (oral or injectable), 0.57 ml (308 mg iodine) in dispenser bottle
	capsule, 200 mg
☐ nicotinamide	tablet, 50 mg
pyridoxine	tablet, 25 mg (hydrochloride)
☐ retinol	sugar-coated tablet, 10 000 IU (as palmitate) (5.5 mg)
	capsule, 200 000 IU (as palmitate) (110 mg)
	oral oily solution, 100 000 IU (as palmitate)/ml in multidose dispenser
	water-miscible injection, 100 000 IU (as palmitate) (55 mg) in 2-ml ampoule
riboflavin	tablet, 5 mg
☐ sodium fluoride	in any appropriate formulation
thiamine	tablet, 50 mg (hydrochloride)

☐ Example of a therapeutic group.

The WHO Model List of Essential Medicines: complementary list

Explanatory notes

The complementary list presents essential medicines for priority diseases which are efficacious, safe and cost-effective but not necessarily affordable, or for which specialized health care facilities or services may be needed.

When the strength of a medicine is specified in terms of a selected salt or ester, this is mentioned in brackets; when it refers to the active moiety, the name of the salt or ester in brackets is preceded by the word "as".

Many medicines included in the Model List are preceded by a square box symbol (□) to indicate that they represent an example of a therapeutic group and that various medicines could serve as alternatives. It is imperative that this is understood when medicines are selected at national level, since choice is then influenced by the comparative cost and availability of equivalent products. Examples of acceptable substitutions include:

— hydrochlorothiazide: any other thiazide-type diuretic currently in broad clinical use;
— hydralazine: any other peripheral vasodilator having an antihypertensive effect;
— senna: any mild stimulant laxative (either synthetic or of plant origin).

Numbers in parentheses following the medicine names indicate:

(1) Medicines subject to international control under: (a) the Single Convention on Narcotic Drugs, 1961 (*21*); (b) the Convention on Psychotropic Substances, 1971 (*22*); or (c) the United Nations Convention against Illicit Traffic in Narcotic Drugs and Psychotropic Substances, 1988 (*23*).
(2) Specific expertise, diagnostic precision, individualization of dosage or special equipment required for proper use.
(3) Greater potency or efficacy.
(4) In renal insufficiency, contraindicated or dosage adjustments necessary.
(5) To improve compliance.
(6) Special pharmacokinetic properties.
(7) Adverse effects diminish benefit/risk ratio.
(8) Limited indications or narrow spectrum of activity.
(9) For epidural anaesthesia.

(10) Sustained-release preparations are available. A proposal to include such a product in a national list of essential medicines should be supported by adequate documentation.

(11) Monitoring of therapeutic concentrations in plasma can improve safety and efficacy.

The letters in parentheses following the medicine names indicate the reasons for the inclusion of the medicine in the complementary list:

(A) When medicines in the core list cannot be made available.

(B) When medicines in the core list are known to be ineffective or inappropriate for a given individual.

(C) For use in rare disorders or in exceptional circumstances.

(D) Reserve antimicrobials to be used only when there is significant resistance to other medicines on the list.

Medicines are grouped according to therapeutic categories. The numbers preceding the sections and subsections have, in general, been allocated in accordance with English alphabetical order; they have no formal significance. Within sections, medicines are listed in alphabetical order.

Certain pharmacological effects have many therapeutic uses. Medicines with multiple uses could be listed under several therapeutic categories in the Model List. However, the inclusion of such medicines in more than one therapeutic category has been limited to those circumstances that the Expert Committee wishes to emphasize. Medicines in the Model List are therefore not listed in all of the therapeutic categories in which they are of value. Detailed information on the therapeutic use of essential medicines is available in the *WHO model formulary (24)*.

Medicine	Route of administration, dosage forms and strengths

1. Anaesthetics

1.2 *Local anaesthetics*

ephedrine[a] (C) — injection, 30 mg (hydrochloride)/ml in 1-ml ampoule

2. Analgesics, antipyretics, nonsteroidal anti-inflammatory medicines, medicines used to treat gout and disease-modifying agents used in rheumatoid disorders

2.2 *Opioid analgesics*

□ pethidine (A) (1a, 4) — injection, 50 mg (hydrochloride) in 1-ml ampoule

tablet, 50 mg, 100 mg (hydrochloride)

5. Anticonvulsants/antiepileptics

□ clonazepam (B) (1b) — scored tablet, 500 µg

6. Anti-infective medicines

6.1 *Anthelminthics*

6.1.2 *Antifilarials*

suramin sodium (B) (2, 7) — powder for injection, 1 g in vial

6.1.3 *Antischistosomals and other antitrematode medicines*

oxamniquine (C) (8) — capsule, 250 mg

syrup, 250 mg/5 ml

6.2 *Antibacterials*

6.2.1 *β-Lactam medicines*

□ amoxicillin + □clavulanic acid[b] (D) — tablet, 500 mg + 125 mg

ceftazidime[b] (D) — powder for injection, 250 mg (as pentahydrate) in vial

□ ceftriaxone[b] (D) — powder for injection, 250 mg (as sodium salt) in vial

imipenem + cilastatin[b] (D) — powder for injection, 250 mg (as monohydrate) + 250 mg (as sodium salt), 500 mg (as monohydrate) + 500 mg (as sodium salt) in vial

---

[a] For use in spinal anaesthesia during delivery, to prevent hypotension.
[b] Reserve antimicrobial for use only when there is significant resistance to other medicines on the Model List.
□ Example of a therapeutic group.

Medicine	Route of administration, dosage forms and strengths

6. Anti-infective medicines (continued)

6.2 Antibacterials (continued)

6.2.2 Other antibacterials

chloramphenicol (C)	oily suspension for injection, 0.5 g (as sodium succinate)/ml in 2-ml ampoule
clindamycin (B) (8)	capsule, 150 mg
	injection, 150 mg (as phosphate)/ml
vancomycin[a] (D)	powder for injection, 250 mg (as hydrochloride) in vial

6.2.4 Antituberculosis medicines

amikacin[b] (D)	powder for injection, 1 g in vial
p-aminosalicylic acid[b] (D)	tablet, 500 mg
	granules, 4 g in sachet
capreomycin[b] (D)	powder for injection, 1 g in vial
ciprofloxacin[b] (D)	tablet, 250 mg, 500 mg
□ cycloserine[b] (D)	capsule or tablet, 250 mg
□ ethionamide[b] (D)	tablet, 125 mg, 250 mg
kanamycin[b] (D)	powder for injection, 1 g in vial
levofloxacin[b] (D)	tablet, 250 mg, 500 mg
ofloxacin[b] (D)	tablet, 200 mg, 400 mg
thioacetazone + isoniazid (A) (5, 7)	tablet, 50 mg + 100 mg, 150 mg + 300 mg

6.3 Antifungal medicines

flucytosine (B) (4, 8)	capsule, 250 mg
	infusion, 2.5 g in 250 ml
potassium iodide (A)	saturated solution

6.5 Antiprotozoal medicines

6.5.2 Antileishmaniasis medicines

amphotericin B (B) (4)	powder for injection, 50 mg in vial

---

[a] Reserve antimicrobial for use only when there is significant resistance to other medicines on the Model List.

[b] Reserve second-line medicine for the treatment of multidrug-resistant tuberculosis which should be used in specialized centres adhering to WHO standards for tuberculosis control.

□ Example of a therapeutic group.

Medicine	Route of administration, dosage forms and strengths

6. Anti-infective medicines (*continued*)

6.5 *Antiprotozoal medicines* (*continued*)

6.5.3 *Antimalarial medicines*

(a) For curative treatment

☐ doxycycline[a] (B) — capsule or tablet, 100 mg (hydrochloride)

mefloquine (B) — tablet, 250 mg (as hydrochloride)

☐ sulfadoxine + pyrimethamine (B) — tablet, 500 mg + 25 mg

artemether[b] (D) — injection, 80 mg/ml in 1-ml ampoule

artesunate[b] (D) — tablet, 50 mg

6.5.5 *Antitrypanosomal medicines*

(a) African trypanosomiasis

eflornithine (C) — injection, 200 mg (hydrochloride)/ml in 100-ml bottle

8. Antineoplastics, immunosuppressives and medicines used in palliative care

8.1 *Immunosuppressive medicines*

Adequate resources and specialist oversight are a prerequisite for this class of medicines.

☐ azathioprine (2) — tablet, 50 mg

powder for injection, 100 mg (as sodium salt) in vial

☐ ciclosporin[c] (2) — capsule, 25 mg

concentrate for injection, 50 mg/ml in 1-ml ampoule

8.2 *Cytotoxic medicines*

Adequate resources and specialist oversight are a prerequisite for this class of medicines.

asparaginase (2) — powder for injection, 10 000 IU in vial

---

[a] For use only in combination with quinine.
[b] Reserve antimicrobial for use only when there is significant resistance to other medicines on the Model List.
[c] For organ transplantation.
☐ Example of a therapeutic group.

Medicine	Route of administration, dosage forms and strengths

8. Antineoplastics, immunosuppressives and medicines used in palliative care (continued)

8.2 Cytotoxic medicines (continued)

bleomycin (2)	powder for injection, 15 mg (as sulfate) in vial
calcium folinate (2)	tablet, 15 mg
	injection, 3 mg/ml in 10-ml ampoule
chlorambucil (2)	tablet, 2 mg
chlormethine (2)	powder for injection, 10 mg (hydrochloride) in vial
cisplatin (2)	powder for injection, 10 mg, 50 mg in vial
cyclophosphamide (2)	tablet, 25 mg
	powder for injection, 500 mg in vial
cytarabine (2)	powder for injection, 100 mg in vial
dacarbazine (2)	powder for injection, 100 mg in vial
dactinomycin (2)	powder for injection, 500 µg in vial
daunorubicin (2)	powder for injection, 50 mg (as hydrochloride)
▯ doxorubicin (2)	powder for injection, 10 mg, 50 mg (hydrochloride) in vial
etoposide (2)	capsule, 100 mg
	injection, 20 mg/ml in 5-ml ampoule
fluorouracil (2)	injection, 50 mg/ml in 5-ml ampoule
levamisole (2)	tablet, 50 mg (as hydrochloride)
mercaptopurine (2)	tablet, 50 mg
methotrexate (2)	tablet, 2.5 mg (as sodium salt)
	powder for injection, 50 mg (as sodium salt) in vial
procarbazine	capsule, 50 mg (as hydrochloride)
vinblastine (2)	powder for injection, 10 mg (sulfate) in vial
vincristine (2)	powder for injection, 1 mg, 5 mg (sulfate) in vial

▯ Example of a therapeutic group.

8. Antineoplastics, immunosuppressives and medicines used in palliative care (*continued*)

8.3 *Hormones and antihormones*

□ prednisolone	tablet, 5 mg
	powder for injection, 20 mg, 25 mg (as sodium phosphate or sodium succinate) in vial
tamoxifen	tablet, 10 mg, 20 mg (as citrate)

8.4 *Medicines used in palliative care*

The Committee recommended that all the medicines mentioned in the WHO publication, *Cancer pain relief: with a guide to opioid availability*, 2nd ed. (*26*), be considered essential. These medicines are included in the relevant sections of the Model List, according to their therapeutic use, e.g. as analgesics.

10. Medicines affecting the blood

10.1 *Antianaemia medicines*

□ iron dextran (B) (5)	injection, equivalent to 50 mg iron/ml in 2-ml ampoule

11. Blood products and plasma substitutes

11.2 *Plasma fractions for specific uses*

All plasma fractions should comply with the Requirements for the Collection, Processing and Quality Control of Blood, Blood Components and Plasma Derivatives (Revised 1992) as published in the forty-third report of the WHO Expert Committee on Biological Standardization (*28*).

□ factor VIII concentrate (C) (2, 8)	dried
□ factor IX complex (coagulation factors II, VII, IX, X) concentrate (C) (2, 8)	dried

12. Cardiovascular medicines

12.2 *Antiarrhythmic medicines*

epinephrine (adrenaline) (C)	injection, 1 mg (as hydrochloride)/ml in ampoule
isoprenaline (C)	injection, 20 µg (hydrochloride)/ml in ampoule

---

□ Example of a therapeutic group.

Medicine	Route of administration, dosage forms and strengths

12. Cardiovascular medicines (*continued*)

12.2 *Antiarrhythmic medicines* (*continued*)

☐ procainamide (B) — injection, 100 mg (hydrochloride)/ml in 10-ml ampoule

☐ quinidine (A) (7) — tablet, 200 mg (sulfate)

12.3 *Antihypertensive medicines*

☐ prazosin (B) — tablet, 500 μg, 1 mg

☐ sodium nitroprusside (C) (2, 8) — powder for infusion, 50 mg in ampoule

12.5 *Antithrombotic medicines*

streptokinase (C) — powder for injection, 100 000 IU, 750 000 IU in vial

13. Dermatological medicines (topical)

13.1 *Antifungal medicines*

selenium sulfide (C) — detergent-based suspension, 2%

13.7 *Ultraviolet-blocking agents*

topical sun protection agent with activity against ultraviolet A and ultraviolet B (C) — cream, lotion or gel

14. Diagnostic agents

14.2 *Radiocontrast media*

☐ meglumine iotroxate (C) — solution, 5–8 g iodine in 100–250 ml

16. Diuretics

☐ mannitol (C) — injectable solution, 10%, 20%

18. Hormones, other endocrine medicines and contraceptives

18.1 *Adrenal hormones and synthetic substitutes*

fludrocortisone (C) — tablet, 100 μg (acetate)

18.2 *Androgens*

testosterone (C) (2) — injection, 200 mg (enantate) in 1-ml ampoule

---

☐ Example of a therapeutic group.

Medicine	Route of administration, dosage forms and strengths

18. Hormones, other endocrine medicines and contraceptives (*continued*)

18.3 *Contraceptives*

18.3.1 Hormonal contraceptives

levonorgestrel (B)	tablet, 30 µg
medroxyprogesterone acetate (B) (7, 8)	depot injection, 150 mg/ml in 1-ml vial
norethisterone enantate (B) (7, 8)	oily solution, 200 mg/ml in 1-ml ampoule

18.7 *Progestogens*

medroxyprogesterone acetate (B)	tablet, 5 mg

20. Muscle relaxants (peripherally-acting) and cholinesterase inhibitors

vecuronium (C)	powder for injection, 10 mg (bromide) in vial

21. Ophthalmological preparations

21.5 *Mydriatics*

epinephrine (adrenaline) (A)	solution (eye drops), 2% (as hydrochloride)

25. Medicines acting on the respiratory tract

25.1 *Antiasthmatic medicines*

☐ cromoglicic acid (B)	inhalation (aerosol), 20 mg (sodium salt) per dose

27. Vitamins and minerals

calcium gluconate (C) (2, 8)	injection, 100 mg/ml in 10-ml ampoule

☐ Example of a therapeutic group.

References

1. Hogerzeil HV et al. Impact of an essential drugs programme on availability and rational use of drugs. *Lancet*, 1989, i(8630):141–142.

2. Quick JD et al., eds. *Managing drug supply*, 2nd ed. West Hartford, CT, Kumarian Press, 1997:122–123.

3. *The selection of essential drugs. Report of a WHO Expert Committee.* Geneva, World Health Organization, 1977 (WHO Technical Report Series, No. 615).

4. WHA28.66. Prophylactic and therapeutic substances. In: *Handbook of resolutions and decisions of the World Health Assembly and Executive Board. Volume II, 1973–1984.* Geneva, World Health Organization, 1985:129.

5. *The selection of essential drugs. Second report of a WHO Expert Committee.* Geneva, World Health Organization, 1979 (WHO Technical Report Series, No. 641).

6. *The use of essential drugs. Report of a WHO Expert Committee.* Geneva, World Health Organization, 1983 (WHO Technical Report Series, No. 685).

7. *The use of essential drugs. Model list of essential drugs (fourth revision). Second report of the WHO Expert Committee.* Geneva, World Health Organization, 1985 (WHO Technical Report Series, No. 722).

8. *The use of essential drugs. Model list of essential drugs (fifth list). Third report of the WHO Expert Committee.* Geneva, World Health Organization, 1988 (WHO Technical Report Series, No. 770).

9. *The use of essential drugs. Model list of essential drugs (sixth list). Fourth report of the WHO Expert Committee.* Geneva, World Health Organization, 1990 (WHO Technical Report Series, No. 796).

10. *The use of essential drugs. Model list of essential drugs (seventh list). Fifth report of the WHO Expert Committee.* Geneva, World Health Organization, 1992 (WHO Technical Report Series, No. 825).

11. *The use of essential drugs. Sixth report of the WHO Expert Committee.* Geneva, World Health Organization, 1995 (WHO Technical Report Series, No. 850).

12. *The use of essential drugs. Seventh report of the WHO Expert Committee.* Geneva, World Health Organization, 1997 (WHO Technical Report Series, No. 867).

13. *The use of essential drugs. Eighth report of the WHO Expert Committee.* Geneva, World Health Organization, 1997 (WHO Technical Report Series, No. 882).

14. *The use of essential drugs. Ninth report of the WHO Expert Committee (including the revised Model List of Essential Drugs).* Geneva, World Health Organization, 2000 (WHO Technical Report Series, No. 895).

15. WHO's revised drug strategy. In: *Thirty-ninth World Health Assembly, Geneva, 5–16 May 1986. Volume 1. Resolutions and decisions, and list of participants.* Geneva, World Health Organization, 1986, Annex 5:93–101 (document WHA39/1986/REC/1).

16. *Development of WHO treatment guidelines: recommended process.* Geneva, World Health Organization, 2001 (in preparation).

17. Good manufacturing practices for pharmaceutical products. In: *WHO Expert Committee on Specifications for Pharmaceutical Preparations. Thirty-second report.* Geneva, World Health Organization, 1992, Annex 1 (WHO Technical Report Series, No. 823).

18. *Guide to good prescribing.* Geneva, World Health Organization, 1994 (document WHO/DAP/94.11).

19. **Laing RO, Hogerzeil HV, Ross-Degnan D.** Ten recommendations to improve use of medicines in developing countries. *Health Policy and Planning,* 2001, 16(1):13–20.

20. *Guidelines for ATC classification and DDD assignment,* 5th ed. Oslo, WHO Collaborating Centre for Drug Statistics Methodology, 2001.

21. *Single Convention on Narcotic Drugs, 1961 with amendments 1972.* New York, NY, United Nations, 1972.

22. *Convention on Psychotropic Substances, 1971.* New York, NY, United Nations, 1977.

23. *United Nations Convention against Illicit Traffic in Narcotic Drugs and Psychotropic Substances,* 1988. New York, NY, United Nations, 1991.

24. *WHO model formulary.* Geneva, World Health Organization, 2002.

25. *Scaling up antiretroviral therapy in resource-limited settings: guidelines for a public health approach.* Geneva, World Health Organization, 2002 (available from the Internet at http://www.who.int/hiv/topics/arv/ISBN 9241545674.pdf).

26. *Cancer pain relief: with a guide to opioid availability,* 2nd ed. Geneva, World Health Organization, 1996.

27. Requirements for Tuberculins (Revised 1985). In: *WHO Expert Committee on Biological Standardization. Thirty-sixth report.* Geneva, World Health Organization, 1987, Annex 1 (WHO Technical Report Series, No. 745).

28. Requirements for the Collection, Processing and Quality Control of Blood, Blood Components, and Plasma Derivatives (Revised 1992). In: *WHO Expert Committee on Biological Standardization. Forty-third report.* Geneva, World Health Organization, 1994, Annex 2 (WHO Technical Report Series, No. 840).

29. Requirements for Dried BCG Vaccine (Revised 1985). In: *WHO Expert Committee on Biological Standardization. Thirty-sixth report.* Geneva, World Health Organization, 1987, Annex 2 (WHO Technical Report Series, No. 745).

30. Requirements for Dried BCG Vaccine (Amendment 1987). In: *WHO Expert Committee on Biological Standardization. Thirty-eight report.* Geneva, World Health Organization, 1988, Annex 12 (WHO Technical Report Series, No. 771).

31. Requirements for Diphtheria, Tetanus, Pertussis and Combined Vaccines (Revised 1989). In: *WHO Expert Committee on Biological Standardization. Fortieth report.* Geneva, World Health Organization, 1990, Annex 2 (WHO Technical Report Series, No. 800).

32. Requirements for Hepatitis B Vaccine Prepared from Plasma (Revised 1994). In: *WHO Expert Committee on Biological Standardization. Forty-fifth report.* Geneva, World Health Organization, 1995, Annex 3 (WHO Technical Report Series, No. 858).

33. Requirements for Measles, Mumps and Rubella Vaccines and Combined Vaccine (Live) (Revised 1992). In: *WHO Expert Committee on Biological Standardization. Forty-third report.* Geneva, World Health Organization, 1994, Annex 3 (WHO Technical Report Series, No. 840).

34. Requirements for Measles, Mumps and Rubella Vaccines and Combined Vaccine (Live). In: *WHO Expert Committee on Biological Standardization. Forty-fourth report.* Geneva, World Health Organization, 1994, Note (WHO Technical Report Series, No. 848).

35. Requirements for Poliomyelitis Vaccine (Oral) (Revised 1989). In: *WHO Expert Committee on Biological Standardization. Fortieth report.* Geneva, World Health Organization, 1990, Annex 1 (WHO Technical Report Series, No. 800).

36. Requirements for Poliomyelitis Vaccine (Inactivated) (Revised 1981). In: *WHO Expert Committee on Biological Standardization.* Geneva, World Health Organization, 1982, Annex 2 (WHO Technical Report Series, No. 673).

37. Requirements for Poliomyelitis Vaccine (Inactivated) (Addendum 1985). In: *WHO Expert Committee on Biological Standardization. Thirty-sixth report.* Geneva, World Health Organization, 1987, Annex 4 (WHO Technical Report Series, No. 745).

38. Requirements for Influenza Vaccine (Inactivated) (Revised 1990). In: *WHO Expert Committee on Biological Standardization. Forty-first report.* Geneva, World Health Organization, 1991, Annex 2 (WHO Technical Report Series, No. 814).

39. Requirements for Meningococcal Polysaccharide Vaccine. In: *WHO Expert Committee on Biological Standardization.* Geneva, World Health Organization, 1976, Annex 2 (WHO Technical Report Series, No. 594).

40. Requirements for Meningococcal Polysaccharide Vaccine (Addendum 1980, incorporating Addendum 1976 and Addendum 1977). In: *WHO Expert Committee on Biological Standardization. Thirty-first report.* Geneva, World Health Organization, 1981, Annex 6 (WHO Technical Report Series, No. 658).

41. Requirements for Rabies Vaccine for Human Use (Revised 1980). In: *WHO Expert Committee on Biological Standardization. Thirty-first report.* Geneva, World Health Organization, 1981, Annex 2 (WHO Technical Report Series, No. 658).

42. Requirements for Rabies Vaccine for Human Use (Amendment 1992). In: *WHO Expert Committee on Biological Standardization. Forty-third report.* Geneva, World Health Organization, 1994, Annex 4 (WHO Technical Report Series, No. 840).

43. Requirements for Rabies Vaccine (Inactivated) for Human Use Produced in Continuous Cell Lines (Revised 1986). In: *WHO Expert Committee on*

Biological Standardization. Thirty-seventh report. Geneva, World Health Organization, 1987, Annex 9 (WHO Technical Report Series, No. 760).

44. Requirements for Rabies Vaccine (Inactivated) for Human Use Produced in Continuous Cell Lines (Amendment 1992). In: *WHO Expert Committee on Biological Standardization. Forty-third report.* Geneva, World Health Organization, 1994, Annex 5 (WHO Technical Report Series, No. 840).

45. Requirements for Typhoid Vaccine (Live, Attenuated, Ty 21a, Oral). In: *WHO Expert Committee on Biological Standardization.* Geneva, World Health Organization, 1984, Annex 3 (WHO Technical Report Series, No. 700).

46. Requirements for Vi Polysaccharide Typhoid Vaccine. In: *WHO Expert Committee on Biological Standardization. Forty-third report.* Geneva, World Health Organization, 1994, Annex 1 (WHO Technical Report Series, No. 840).

47. Requirements for Yellow Fever Vaccine (Revised 1995). In: *WHO Expert Committee on Biological Standardization. Forty-sixth report.* Geneva, World Health Organization, 1998, Annex 2 (WHO Technical Report Series, No. 872).

Appendix 1

Information to be included with an application for the inclusion, change or deletion of a medicine in the WHO Model List of Essential Medicines

1. Summary statement of the proposal for inclusion, change or deletion.
2. Name of the focal point within WHO submitting or supporting the application.
3. Name of the organization(s) consulted and/or supporting the application.
4. International Nonproprietary Name (INN, generic name) of the medicine.
5. Whether listing is requested as an individual medicine or as an example of a therapeutic group.
6. Information supporting the public health relevance (e.g. epidemiological information on disease burden, assessment of current use, target population).
7. Treatment details (i.e. dosage regimen and duration; reference to existing WHO and other clinical guidelines; need for special diagnostic or treatment facilities and skills).
8. Summary of comparative effectiveness in a variety of clinical settings, including:
   — identification of clinical evidence (i.e. search strategy, systematic reviews identified, reasons for selection/exclusion of particular data);
   — summary of available data (i.e. appraisal of quality, outcome measures, summary of results);
   — summary of available estimates of comparative effectiveness.
9. Summary of comparative evidence on safety, including:
   — estimate of total patient exposure to date;
   — description of adverse effects/reactions;
   — identification of variation in safety due to health systems and patient factors;
   — summary of comparative safety against comparators.

10. Summary of available data on comparative cost[1] and cost-effectiveness within the pharmacological class or therapeutic group, including:
    — range of costs of the proposed medicine;
    — comparative cost-effectiveness presented as range of cost per routine outcome (e.g. cost per case, cost per cure, cost per month of treatment, cost per case prevented, cost per clinical event prevented, or, if possible and relevant, cost per quality-adjusted life year gained).
11. Summary of regulatory status of the medicine (in country of origin, and preferably in other countries as well).
12. Availability of pharmacopoeial standards (*British pharmacopoeia, The international pharmacopoeia, United States pharmacopoeia*).
13. Proposed (new/adapted) text for the *WHO model formulary*.

Applications for additions and changes to, or deletions from, the Model List of Essential Medicines should be sent to: The Secretary of the Expert Committee on the Selection and Use of Essential Medicines, Department of Essential Drugs and Medicines Policy, World Health Organization, 1211 Geneva 27, Switzerland.

---

[1] Information on cost and cost-effectiveness should preferably refer to average generic world market prices as listed in the *International Drug Price Indicator Guide*, an essential medicines pricing service provided by WHO and maintained by Management Sciences for Health. If this information is not available, other international sources, such as the WHO, UNICEF and *Médecins sans Frontières* price information service, can be used. All cost analyses should specify the source of the price information.

Annex 2
Additional notes on the medicines recommended for inclusion in the 12th WHO Model List of Essential Medicines

Antiretroviral medicines

Evidence provided to the WHO Expert Committee on the Selection and Use of Essential Medicines in support of the application to include 12 antiretroviral (ARV) medicines in the Model List of Essential Medicines was assembled from a series of literature searches, some of which were conducted by staff at the Cochrane Collaboration. For review purposes, the Expert Committee classified this evidence as follows:

- Level 1. Evidence from relevant high quality systematic reviews of unbiased randomized comparative clinical trials.
- Level 2. Evidence from at least one relevant unbiased randomized comparative clinical trial.
- Level 3. Evidence from relevant controlled observational studies.

Nucleoside reverse transcriptase inhibitors

The medicines proposed for listing were zidovudine (ZDV or AZT), lamivudine (3TC), stavudine (d4T), didanosine (ddI) and abacavir (ABC). Typically, two of the first four agents are used to assemble a dual nucleoside "core" to which a third agent, abacavir, a non-nucleoside reverse transcriptase inhibitor or a protease inhibitor, is added. The most commonly used dual nucleoside core is the combination, zidovudine + lamivudine (ZDV + 3TC).

Zidovudine + lamivudine

The literature search retrieved a large number of citations that described randomized controlled trials involving zidovudine + lamivudine, used as a dual nucleoside therapy or in combination with a range of other ARV agents. Of these, 3 meta-analyses and 11 randomized controlled trials provided comparative information on the performance of zidovudine + lamivudine relative to the alternative dual nucleoside regimens that are recommended in the WHO guidelines for ARVs (1); these studies were considered to constitute Level 1 and Level 2 evidence of efficacy.

The trials provided not only unambiguous evidence of the efficacy of zidovudine + lamivudine as a dual nucleoside core (which could be combined with a range of other ARVs), but also data which established the efficacy of the alternative regimens recommended in the WHO guidelines for ARVs (1). More specifically, several studies showed that the efficacy of zidovudine + lamivudine was similar to that of other commonly used dual nucleoside regimens. According to one large direct comparative study, the fixed-dose combination of zidovudine + lamivudine was as effective as the concomitant use of the individual medicines. However, the fixed-dose combination resulted in a higher level of adherence to the prescribed treatment regimen.

The trials also indicated that the combination was fairly well tolerated, although, qualitatively, the nature of the adverse reactions observed tended to vary between the different nucleoside combinations. In general, nausea, anaemia, neutropenia and thrombocytopenia were more common in patients receiving zidovudine-containing regimens, while neuropathic symptoms, and possibly lactic acidosis, were more likely to occur in patients taking other nucleoside combinations.

Stavudine
Nineteen randomized trials involving stavudine were retrieved by the literature search; in nine of these, stavudine was used as part of a three-medicine combination. Results of these trials were considered to constitute Level 2 evidence of efficacy.

Of those studies in which stavudine was combined with another nucleoside reverse transcriptase inhibitor in order to form a dual nucleoside core, five involved didanosine as the other medicine and in three, lamivudine was the second nucleoside reverse transcriptase inhibitor. In direct comparisons of dual nucleoside regimens that are generally considered to be effective, stavudine + didanosine was found to be either equivalent or superior to zidovudine + lamivudine in terms of efficacy; moreover, the dual combination was as well tolerated as zidovudine + lamivudine. Stavudine was also found to be effective when combined with lamivudine; when used in combinations comprising three or more medicines, the pairing stavudine + lamivudine demonstrated an efficacy similar to that of stavudine + didanosine. The combination, stavudine + zidovudine, was not especially effective in trials and thus stavudine was not recommended for use in combination with this particular ARV by the Committee.

Overall, the combination stavudine + didanosine was reasonably well tolerated; although pancreatitis occurred more frequently in patients taking this combination compared with those on zidovudine + lamivudine, the latter was more likely to cause anaemia.

Didanosine

Sixteen randomized trials involving didanosine were reviewed, including five studies in which didanosine + stavudine was used as part of a three-medicine combination. These studies were considered to provide Level 2 evidence of efficacy.

In direct comparisons of dual nucleoside regimens that are considered effective, the combination didanosine + stavudine was found to be either as effective as or more effective than, and also as well tolerated as, the combination, zidovudine + lamivudine. When tested as part of a three-medicine combination, didanosine + stavudine in combination with indinavir was found to be as effective as, or more effective than, zidovudine + lamivudine + indinavir and as effective as stavudine + lamivudine + indinavir.

Generally, the combination, didanosine + stavudine + indinavir, was fairly well tolerated. Patients receiving the didanosine + stavudine combination were more likely to develop pancreatitis whereas anaemia was the more commonly observed complication associated with the use of zidovudine + lamivudine combinations.

Abacavir

Abacavir is usually used as a third medicine to complement dual nucleoside therapy and, as such, is used in an equivalent fashion to the non-nucleoside reverse transcriptase inhibitors and the protease inhibitors. Library searches conducted by the Cochrane Review Group for HIV/AIDS produced a total of seven randomized controlled trials and five uncontrolled single arm studies that collectively provided an insight into the efficacy and safety of abacavir for different indications. These studies were considered to constitute Level 2 and Level 3 evidence of efficacy.

In three of the controlled trials, abacavir was used as a component of an initial therapy regimen in ARV-naïve subjects. When used in this way, the efficacy of the three-medicine combination, abacavir + zidovudine + lamivudine, was reported to be superior to that of the two nucleoside reverse transcriptase inhibitors alone. Other studies have demonstrated that abacavir-containing regimens are equivalent to protease inhibitor-containing regimens in achieving viral suppression, with the possible exception of subjects with high baseline viral loads. Furthermore, there was some evidence to suggest that the use of combinations that include abacavir as opposed to protease inhibitors may lead to improved adherence to prescribed treatment regimens.

The effect of the addition of abacavir (relative to a placebo) was studied in patients with viral loads above 400 counts/ml who were receiving dual and triple-medicine regimens (i.e. intensification therapy). Overall, the trial showed that patients on abacavir were more likely to have a viral load of less than 400 counts/ml after 48 weeks of therapy than those taking the placebo. 13% of patients in the abacavir arm had viral loads that were less than 50 counts/ml; in comparison, none of the patients receiving the placebo had viral loads as low as 50 counts/ml. The remaining three trials examined the role of abacavir as an alternative to protease inhibitors (i.e. as replacement therapy) in patients receiving stable combined drug therapy. Results of all three revealed high rates of continued viral suppression in patients randomized to abacavir-based regimens.

The trials indicated that, overall, abacavir is tolerated reasonably well. Rates of adverse reactions were similar to, or less than, those observed in patients receiving protease inhibitor-containing regimens and treatment adherence rates were similar or higher. However, hypersensitivity reactions were associated with the use of abacavir in several trials, with reported rates varying between 2% and 10%. Such reactions were occasionally severe and several fatalities have been recorded. This finding highlighted the importance of proper training for health-care providers, in particular, with regard to the identification of early symptoms and signs of abacavir hypersensitivity reactions.

Abacavir is currently available as part of a fixed-dose combination product, comprising abacavir, lamivudine and zidovudine.

Non-nucleoside reverse transcriptase inhibitors

Two non-nucleoside reverse transcriptase inhibitors were proposed for listing: nevirapine (NVP) and efavirenz (EFV or EFZ). These medicines are usually added as a third agent to dual nucleoside core combinations.

Nevirapine
Library searches compiled in collaboration with the Cochrane Review Group for HIV/AIDS resulted in the retrieval of a substantial number of randomized controlled trials and five uncontrolled single arm studies involving nevirapine. These studies were classified as Level 2 and Level 3 evidence of efficacy.

Several of the randomized controlled trials were included in a published meta-analysis that documented a clear advantage of using nevirapine in combination with two nucleoside reverse transcriptase inhibitors over dual nucleoside therapy alone. The meta-analysis also demonstrated that combinations comprising nevirapine plus two nucleoside reverse transcriptase inhibitors were as effective, but possibly better tolerated, than highly active ARV therapies that included a protease inhibitor. Randomized trials not included in the meta-analysis provided further evidence in support of the benefits of nevirapine-containing regimens, which include once-daily dosing, an improved quality of life and a regression in lipid abnormalities.

As the combination, nevirapine + stavudine + lamivudine, has been the subject of only one randomized clinical trial, information from uncontrolled studies was used to evaluate this particular regimen. On the whole, such data supported the efficacy of this regimen. Evidence reviewed by the Committee for other ARV combinations, indicated that the stavudine + lamivudine nucleoside pair is as effective as the more widely used combination, zidovudine + lamivudine.

The principal adverse effect associated with the use of nevirapine was rash. In most trials, rash occurred in at least 20% of individuals; such rates are higher than those typically observed with the other ARVs. Nevertheless, withdrawal from therapy because of adverse drug reactions (ADRs) was not noticeably more prevalent among patients taking nevirapine than those on other ARVs. Whereas severe liver damage has been reported in some patients on other ARVs, it has been observed only rarely with nevirapine. Risk factors for the development of liver damage with ARVs include heavy alcohol use and co-infection with hepatitis C virus (HCV). Although the rare occurrence of severe liver toxicity is a legitimate concern when using nevirapine in post-exposure prophylaxis (a low-risk situation), the evidence reviewed on this occasion was considered insufficient to warrant discouraging its use in individuals who are infected with HIV.

Efavirenz

Library searches conducted by the Cochrane Review Group for HIV/AIDS generated a total of 15 good quality randomized clinical trials involving efavirenz. These were considered to constitute Level 2 evidence of efficacy.

When used in initial therapy (six trials), the action of efavirenz in combination with two nucleoside reverse transcriptase inhibitors (zidovudine + lamivudine in five of the six trials) was superior to that of the two nucleoside reverse transcriptase inhibitors alone. Efavirenz-containing regimens were as good as, or better than, protease inhibitor-containing regimens in achieving long-term viral suppression, but efavirenz-containing regimens that lacked nucleoside reverse transcriptase inhibitors were inferior to those that contained them.

The efficacy of efavirenz as a component of salvage therapy in failing regimens was examined in 5 of the 15 trials. These studies showed that efavirenz was an effective medicine for non-nucleoside reverse transcriptase inhibitor-naïve patients who were failing nucleoside reverse transcriptase inhibitor regimens. In such cases, regimens comprising efavirenz plus a protease inhibitor (either nelfinavir or indinavir) were superior to efavirenz given alone and also to a single protease inhibitor.

Efavirenz has also been tested (the remaining four trials) as an alternative to protease inhibitors in patients who are susceptible to the lipodystrophy syndrome that can be induced by these medicines (i.e. switch therapy). The three trials for which data were available showed that use of efavirenz in place of continued treatment with protease inhibitors resulted in comparable or superior viral suppression. These studies also demonstrated that efavirenz was as efficacious as nevirapine and abacavir in maintaining viral suppression but was more likely to be associated with hypercholesterolemia and hypertriglyceridemia.

Overall, efavirenz was tolerated quite well. Although certain side effects were common (e.g. rash, central nervous system effects including dizziness, impaired concentration and dreaming), rates of discontinuation because of toxicity were the same as, or lower than, those reported in patients using combination therapies that included protease inhibitors.

Protease inhibitors

Protease inhibitors, like the non-nucleoside reverse transcriptase inhibitors, are usually added as a third agent to a dual nucleoside core combination. When used in such combinations, these medicines are amongst the most potent suppressors of HIV replication. For this reason, they are generally reserved for use later in the course of a patient's treatment.

Five protease inhibitors were proposed for listing: nelfinavir (NFV), indinavir (IDV), lopinavir (LPV), ritonavir(r) and saquinavir (SQV). Ritonavir is often used at relatively low doses in combination with indinavir, lopinavir and saquinavir as a booster and not as a protease inhibitor in its own right. At low doses, ritonavir inhibits the metabolism of the companion protease inhibitor, greatly enhancing the latter's bioavailability. When used in this manner, low-dose ritonavir allows the frequency of protease inhibitor dosing to be decreased and reduces the need for dietary restrictions that are otherwise associated with the use of protease inhibitors. For effective protease inhibition, much higher doses of ritonavir would be needed than those recommended in the present Model List.

Nelfinavir
Twelve randomized controlled clinical trials of nelfinavir were recovered by the literature search. Collectively, these trials evaluated a total of 21 treatment arms, 11 of which involved the use of nelfinavir as a part of triple therapy and 9 involved the use of nelfinavir in combination with two nucleoside reverse transcriptase inhibitors. These studies were considered to constitute Level 2 evidence of efficacy.

In these clinical trials, nelfinavir-containing combinations displayed similar efficacy to other protease inhibitor-containing medicine combinations, with some evidence of superior tolerability. The most common adverse effect was diarrhoea.

Indinavir + low-dose ritonavir
Library searches compiled by the Cochrane Review Group for HIV/AIDS produced a number of studies documenting the nature of the pharmacokinetic interaction between indinavir and ritonavir. These studies confirmed that the interaction between indinavir and ritonavir results in higher minimum concentrations of indinavir which, in turn, allow the combination treatment to be given twice daily (as opposed to three times daily when indinavir is used alone) and without dietary restrictions.

At full treatment doses, indinavir is known to be an effective protease inhibitor and when used in combination with other medicines — usually two nucleoside reverse transcriptase inhibitors — to have a potent antiretroviral action. Studies on the effect of indinavir in combination with a dual nucleoside core were reviewed as part of the submissions for the nucleoside reverse transcriptase inhibitors (e.g. see Didanosine).

Studies involving the use of indinavir in combination with low doses of ritonavir are, however, limited in number. The literature search revealed only one randomized clinical trial (which compared the efficacy of indinavir + low-dose ritonavir (IDV/r) given twice daily with that of full-dose indinavir treatment three times daily), one non-randomized comparative study and seven uncontrolled studies, that is to say, predominantly Level 3 evidence of efficacy.

In all of these studies, the protease inhibitor combination was given together with other ARV agents, usually two nucleoside reverse transcriptase inhibitors. The results provided some evidence to suggest that, over the range of different doses of indinavir and ritonavir tested, the indinavir + low-dose ritonavir combination is as efficacious as indinavir at full dosages (1). As it was not clear whether indinavir + low-dose ritonavir combination therapy was associated with fewer adverse side effects than full-dose indinavir, it would be prudent to assume that, in this respect at least, the former combination offers no real advantage. The convenience of twice-daily therapy is, however, a clear advantage.

At present, indinavir + low-dose ritonavir is not available as a fixed-dose combination.

Lopinavir + low-dose ritonavir
Lopinavir + low-dose ritonavir (LPV/r) is an extremely potent protease inhibitor. Library searches performed by the Cochrane Review Group for HIV/AIDS recovered details of five randomized clinical trials involving lopinavir + low-dose ritonavir which were considered to constitute Level 2 evidence of efficacy.

In three of the five trials, lopinavir + low-dose ritonavir in combination with two nucleoside reverse transcriptase inhibitors (typically stavudine + lamivudine) achieved high rates of viral suppression in ARV-naïve subjects. Lopinavir + low-dose ritonavir, in a single dose, was reported to be as effective as lopinavir given twice daily, and when administered in combination with stavudine + lamivudine, was superior to a corresponding nelfinavir-containing combination. The two remaining trials demonstrated the potency of lopinavir + low-dose ritonavir as a rescue therapy in subjects who had increased viral loads despite treatment with multiple ARVs.

Lopinavir + low-dose ritonavir is currently available as a fixed-dose combination from two manufacturers.

Saquinavir + low-dose ritonavir
The Cochrane Review Group for HIV/AIDS who conducted the library search for studies involving saquinavir + low-dose ritonavir (SQV/r), retrieved details of six randomized clinical trials which were considered to represent Level 2 evidence of efficacy.

Across the six trials, the most commonly used regimen was 400 mg of each medicine, twice daily, although different doses of the two medicines were also tested. One trial documented an apparent therapeutic equivalence of a range of doses of the two medicines when combined with two nucleoside reverse transcriptase inhibitors. However, the 400 mg + 400 mg dose, being the lowest total dose of the medicines and also the dose with the best tolerance, was considered to be the most attractive option. In another large trial, the efficacy of saquinavir + low-dose ritonavir at a dose of 400 mg + 400 mg was compared with that of indinavir or ritonavir given in full doses; results indicated that the saquinavir + low-dose ritonavir combination was at least as effective overall and more effective in patients who had not been previously treated with ARVs than the single medicines. Although the remaining trials provided some additional insight into the potential of this particular combination, their usefulness for assessment purposes was impaired by a number of inherent study design shortcomings. For example, several trials involved suboptimal saquinavir + low-dose ritonavir combinations (e.g. saquinavir + low-dose ritonavir in combination with only one nucleoside reverse transcriptase inhibitor); another compared the saquinavir-containing regimen with one that is not recommended in the WHO guidelines (1). Overall, however, the evidence was considered to be of reasonable quality and probably better than that which supports the combined use of indinavir + low-dose ritonavir.

Adverse effects were broadly similar to those observed with other protease inhibitor combinations, but without the problems of nephrolithiasis, an effect that is typically linked to the use of indinavir.

Artemether + lumefantrine (fixed-dose combination)

WHO recommends that when used for the treatment of acute uncomplicated multidrug-resistant falciparum malaria, artemisinin and its derivatives should be administered in combination with another effective blood schizontocide in order to reduce recrudescences and to slow the development of resistance (2). Such artemisinin-based combinations, which include artesunate + mefloquine and artemether + lumefantrine, have several distinct advantages over other antimalarials in that: (i) they are capable of producing a rapid clinical and parasitological cure; (ii) as yet there is no documented parasite resistance to them; (iii) they reduce gametocyte carrier rates; and (iv) they are generally well tolerated. At present, only ad hoc combinations of artesunate + mefloquine are used operationally for the treatment of acute falciparum malaria in areas of multidrug resistance. In such settings, fixed-dose combinations would have a number of practical advantages over the ad hoc combinations, including ease of use and improved adherence to treatment regimens in the target populations.

At present, artemether + lumefantrine is the only artemisinin-based fixed-dose combination that has been both widely studied and registered for the treatment of acute multidrug-resistant falciparum malaria. It has been shown to be an efficacious and safe formulation when used for the treatment of acute uncomplicated falciparum malaria in Africa, China and Thailand. Studies in Thailand, for example, have demonstrated that artemether + lumefantrine provides similar cure rates to artesunate + mefloquine in areas prone to multidrug-resistant falciparum malaria and, as such, has the potential to serve as a suitable alternative to artesunate + mefloquine in these areas.

At its meeting in 1999, the Committee rejected a proposal to add the fixed-dose combination, artemether + lumefantrine, to the Model List on a number of grounds, including lack of data on operational use and concerns about compliance and cost (see section 6.1.2). These issues have now been addressed as follows:

- Operational experience. Due to unacceptable levels of resistance to sulfadoxine + pyrimethamine in the region, KwaZulu Natal developed a malaria treatment policy based on the use of artemether + lumefantrine as its first-level medicine. The policy, the first of its kind to be adopted by a department of health in Africa, was implemented in February 2001 in conjunction with improved vector control measures. At the end of 2001, a dramatic 78% reduction in the total number of malaria cases (from 41 786 cases in 2000 to 9443 cases in 2001) and an 87% decrease in the number of malaria deaths was recorded. This impressive improvement in the malaria situation was attributed to the combined effects of the increased use of residual household spraying and the replacement of an ineffective malaria treatment by the fixed-dose combination, artemether + lumefantrine.

- Compliance. In household surveys conducted following the introduction of the above policy in KwaZulu Natal, 95.4% of patients surveyed claimed that they had completed their course of treatment with artemether + lumefantrine and only 0.5% admitted that they had medicines remaining at home. The corresponding figures for Mpumalanga were 86.6% and 1.3%, respectively. New packaging designed to improve compliance in patients of low literary status has been developed and its effectiveness is currently being assessed.

WHO clinical guidelines on the use of artemether + lumefantrine, published in 2000, state that a 6-dose regimen should be adopted as the standard for all age groups and in all situations in order to avoid confusion and to ensure the highest efficacy and reliability possible with this combination (2). The manufacturer has agreed to these recommendations. As only the 4-dose regimen has been registered for use in selected malaria-endemic developing countries (mainly in Africa), further studies with the 6-dose regimen are required to support its registration in such countries.

- Prices. The manufacturer has agreed to provide the fixed-dose combination, artemether + lumefantrine, as Coartem® to WHO at a no-profit price. As of February 2002, the price to WHO of the range of treatment doses, based on a 6-dose regimen, are as follows:

  — children 10–14 kg = US$ 0.90;
  — children 15–24 kg = US$ 1.40;
  — children 25–34 kg = US$ 1.90;
  — adult > 35 kg = US$ 2.40.

  These prices are approximately half those presently being charged for the medicine in KwaZulu Natal and equivalent to the lowest available price for the ad hoc combination of artesunate + mefloquine that is currently used in Cambodia. It is anticipated that further reductions in the price of artemether + lumefantrine may be possible in the future for the most vulnerable population groups.

References

1. *Scaling up antiretroviral therapy in resource-limited settings: guidelines for a public health approach.* Geneva, World Health Organization, 2002 (available from the Internet at http://www.who.int/hiv/topics/arv/ISBN 9241945674.pdf).

2. *Guidelines for establishing DOTS-Plus pilot projects for the management of multidrug-resistant tuberculosis (MDR-TB).* Geneva, World Health Organization, 2000 (document WHO/CDS/TB/2000.279).

© World Health Organization
WHO Technical Report Series, No. 914, 2003

Annex 3
The Anatomical Therapeutic Chemical (ATC) classification system[1]

The following list provides the corresponding Anatomical Therapeutic Chemical (ATC) classification codes for all items on the 12th WHO Model List of Essential Medicines, sorted by ATC code number.

ATC code	ATC group/medicine or item
A	**ALIMENTARY TRACT AND METABOLISM**
A02	**Drugs for acid related disorders**
A02A	**Antacids**
A02AA	*Magnesium compounds*
A02AA04	magnesium hydroxide
A02AB	*Aluminium compounds*
A02AB01	aluminium hydroxide
A02B	**Drugs for peptic ulcer and gastro-oesophageal reflux disease (GORD)**
A02BA	*H_2-receptor antagonists*
A02BA01	cimetidine
A03	**Drugs for functional gastrointestinal disorders**
A03B	**Belladonna and derivatives, plain**
A03BA	*Belladonna alkaloids, tertiary amines*
A03BA01	atropine
A03F	**Propulsives**
A03FA	*Propulsives*
A03FA01	metoclopramide
A06	**Laxatives**
A06A	**Laxatives**
A06AB	*Contact laxatives*
A06AB06	senna*
A07	**Antidiarrheals, intestinal antiinflammatory/antiinfective agents**
A07A	**Intestinal antiinfectives**
A07AA	*Antibiotics*
A07AA02	nystatin

---

[1] Based on the ATC list as of January 2002 and prepared by the WHO Collaborating Centre for Drug Statistics Methodology, Oslo, Norway.

ATC code	ATC group/medicine or item

A07B **Intestinal adsorbents**
A07BA *Charcoal preparations*
A07BA01 charcoal, activated*

A07C **Electrolytes with carbohydrates**
A07CA *oral rehydration salts**

A07E **Intestinal antiinflammatory agents**
A07EA *Corticosteroids for local use*
A07EA02 hydrocortisone

A07EC *Aminosalicylic acid and similar agents*
A07EC01 sulfasalazine

A10 **Drugs used in diabetes**
A10A **Insulins and analogues**
A10AB *insulin injection (soluble)**
A10AC *insulin, intermediate-acting**

A10B **Oral blood glucose lowering drugs**
A10BA *Biguanides*
A10BA02 metformin

A10BB *Sulfonamides, urea derivatives*
A10BB01 glibenclamide

A11 **Vitamins**
A11C **Vitamin A and D, incl. combinations of the two**
A11CA *Vitamin A, plain*
A11CA01 retinol

A11CC *Vitamin D and analogues*
A11CC01 ergocalciferol

A11D **Vitamin B_1, plain and in combination with vitamin B_6 and B_{12}**
A11DA *Vitamin B_1, plain*
A11DA01 thiamine

A11G **Ascorbic acid (vitamin C), incl. combinations**
A11GA *Ascorbic acid (vitamin C), plain*
A11GA01 ascorbic acid

A11H **Other plain vitamin preparations**
A11HA *Other plain vitamin preparations*
A11HA01 nicotinamide
A11HA02 pyridoxine
A11HA04 riboflavin

A12 **Mineral supplements**
A12A **Calcium**
A12AA *Calcium*
A12AA03 calcium gluconate

ATC code	ATC group/medicine or item

A12C   **Other mineral supplements**
A12CD   *Fluoride*
A12CD01   sodium fluoride

A12CX   *Other mineral products*
A12CX   iodine*

B   **BLOOD AND BLOOD FORMING ORGANS**
B01   **Antithrombotic agents**
B01A   **Antithrombotic agents**
B01AA   *Vitamin K antagonists*
B01AA03   warfarin

B01AB   *Heparin group*
B01AB01   heparin sodium*

B01AC   *Platelet aggregation inhibitors excl. heparin*
B01AC06   acetylsalicylic acid

B01AD   *Enzymes*
B01AD01   streptokinase

B02   **Antihemorrhagics**
B02B   **Vitamin K and other hemostatics**
B02BA   *Vitamin K*
B02BA01   phytomenadione

B02BD   *Blood coagulation factors*
B02BD01   factor IX complex (coagulation factors II, VII, IX, X) concentrate*
B02BD02   factor VIII concentrate*

B03   **Antianemic preparations**
B03A   **Iron preparations**
B03A   ferrous salt*

B03AC   *Iron trivalent, parenteral preparations*
B03AC06   iron dextran*

B03AD   *ferrous salt + folic acid**

B03B   **Vitamin B_{12} and folic acid**
B03BA   *Vitamin B_{12} (cyanocobalamin and analogues)*
B03BA03   hydroxocobalamin

B03BB   *Folic acid and derivatives*
B03BB01   folic acid

B05   **Blood substitutes and perfusion solutions**
B05A   **Blood and related products**
B05AA   *Blood substitutes and plasma protein fractions*
B05AA05   dextran 70*
B05AA06   polygeline*

ATC code	ATC group/medicine or item
B05B	**I.v. solutions**
B05BA	*Solutions for parenteral nutrition*
B05BA03	glucose*
B05BB	*Solutions affecting the electrolyte balance*
B05BB01	sodium lactate, compound solution*
B05BB02	glucose with sodium chloride*
B05BC	*Solutions producing osmotic diuresis*
B05BC01	mannitol
B05D	**Peritoneal dialytics**
B05DA	*intraperitoneal dialysis solution**
B05X	**I.v. solution additives**
B05XA	*Electrolyte solutions*
B05XA01	potassium chloride
B05XA02	sodium hydrogen carbonate*
B05XA03	sodium chloride
B05XA05	magnesium sulfate
C	**CARDIOVASCULAR SYSTEM**
C01	**Cardiac therapy**
C01A	**Cardiac glycosides**
C01AA	*Digitalis glycosides*
C01AA05	digoxin
C01B	**Antiarrhythmics, class I and III**
C01BA	*Antiarrhythmics, class Ia*
C01BA01	quinidine
C01BA02	procainamide
C01BB	*Antiarrhythmics, class Ib*
C01BB01	lidocaine
C01C	**Cardiac stimulants excl. cardiac glycosides**
C01CA	*Adrenergic and dopaminergic agents*
C01CA04	dopamine
C01CA24	epinephrine
C01D	**Vasodilators used in cardiac diseases**
C01DA	*Organic nitrates*
C01DA02	glyceryl trinitrate
C01DA08	isosorbide dinitrate
C02	**Antihypertensives**
C02A	**Antiadrenergic agents, centrally acting**
C02AA	*Rauwolfia alkaloids*
C02AA02	reserpine
C02AB	*Methyldopa*
C02AB01	methyldopa*

ATC code	ATC group/medicine or item
C02C	**Antiadrenergic agents, peripherally acting**
C02CA	*Alpha-adrenoreceptor antagonists*
C02CA01	prazosin
C02D	**Arteriolar smooth muscle, agents acting on**
C02DB	*Hydrazinophthalazine derivatives*
C02DB02	hydralazine
C02DD	*Nitroferricyanide derivatives*
C02DD01	sodium nitroprusside*
C03	**Diuretics**
C03A	**Low-ceiling diuretics, thiazides**
C03AA	*Thiazides, plain*
C03AA03	hydrochlorothiazide
C03C	**High-ceiling diuretics**
C03CA	*Sulfonamides, plain*
C03CA01	furosemide
C03D	**Potassium-sparing agents**
C03DA	*Aldosterone antagonists*
C03DA01	spironolactone
C03DB	*Other potassium-sparing agents*
C03DB01	amiloride
C05	**Vasoprotectives**
C05A	**Antihemorrhoidals for topical use**
C05A	antihaemorrhoidal preparation: local anaesthetic, astringent, and anti-inflammatory medicine*
C07	**Beta blocking agents**
C07A	**Beta blocking agents**
C07AA	*Beta blocking agents, non-selective*
C07AA05	propranolol
C07AB	*Beta blocking agents, selective*
C07AB03	atenolol
C08	**Calcium channel blockers**
C08C	**Selective calcium channel blockers with mainly vascular effects**
C08CA	*Dihydropyridine derivatives*
C08CA05	nifedipine
C08D	**Selective calcium channel blockers with direct cardiac effects**
C08DA	*Phenylalkylamine derivatives*
C08DA01	verapamil
C09	**Agents acting on the renin-angiotensin system**
C09A	**ACE inhibitors, plain**
C09AA	*ACE inhibitors, plain*
C09AA01	captopril

ATC code	ATC group/medicine or item
D	**DERMATOLOGICALS**
D01	**Antifungals for dermatological use**
D01A	**Antifungals for topical use**
D01AA	*Antibiotics*
D01AA01	nystatin
D01AC	*Imidazole and triazole derivatives*
D01AC02	miconazole
D01AE	*Other antifungals for topical use*
D01AE02	methylrosanilinium chloride (gentian violet)*
D01AE12	salicylic acid
D01AE13	selenium sulfide
D01AE20	benzoic acid + salicylic acid*
D01B	**Antifungals for systemic use**
D01BA	*Antifungals for systemic use*
D01BA01	griseofulvin
D02	**Emollients and protectives**
D02A	**Emollients and protectives**
D02AB	*Zinc products*
D02AB	calamine lotion*
D02AE	*Carbamide products*
D02AE01	urea*
D02B	**Protectives against UV-radiation**
D02BA	*Protectives against UV-radiation for topical use*
D02BA	sun protection agent with activity against ultraviolet A and ultraviolet B*
D05	**Antipsoriatics**
D05A	**Antipsoriatics for topical use**
D05AA	*coal tar**
D05AC	*Antracen derivatives*
D05AC01	dithranol
D06	**Antibiotics and chemotherapeutics for dermatological use**
D06A	**Antibiotics for topical use**
D06AX	*Other antibiotics for topical use*
D06AX04	neomycin + bacitracin*
D06B	**Chemotherapeutics for topical use**
D06BA	*Sulfonamides*
D06BA01	silver sulfadiazine
D06BB	*Antivirals*
D06BB04	podophyllum resin*
D07	**Corticosteroids, dermatological preparations**
D07A	**Corticosteroids, plain**
D07AA	*Corticosteroids, weak (group I)*
D07AA02	hydrocortisone

ATC code	ATC group/medicine or item
D07AC	*Corticosteroids, potent (group III)*
D07AC01	betamethasone
D08	**Antiseptics and disinfectants**
D08A	**Antiseptics and disinfectants**
D08AC	*Biguanides and amidines*
D08AC02	chlorhexidine
D08AE	*Phenol and derivatives*
D08AE05	chloroxylenol
D08AG	*Iodine products*
D08AG02	polyvidone iodine*
D08AL	*Silver compounds*
D08AL01	silver nitrate
D08AX	*Other antiseptics and disinfectants*
D08AX	chlorine base compound*
D08AX06	potassium permanganate
D08AX08	ethanol
D08AX09	glutaral
D10	**Anti-acne preparations**
D10A	**Anti-acne preparations for topical use**
D10AE	*Peroxides*
D10AE01	benzoyl peroxide
D10AX	*Other anti-acne preparations for topical use*
D10AX05	aluminium diacetate
G	**GENITO URINARY SYSTEM AND SEX HORMONES**
G01	**Gynecological antiinfectives and antiseptics**
G01A	**Antiinfectives and antiseptics, excl. combinations with corticosteroids**
G01AA	*Antibiotics*
G01AA01	nystatin
G02	**Other gynecologicals**
G02A	**Oxytocics**
G02AB	*Ergot alkaloids*
G02AB03	ergometrine
G02B	**Contraceptives for topical use**
G02BA	*Intrauterine contraceptives*
G02BA02	copper-containing intrauterine device*
G02BB	*Intravaginal contraceptives*
G02BB	diaphragms with spermicide (nonoxinol)*
G03	**Sex hormones and modulators of the genital system**
G03A	**Hormonal contraceptives for systemic use**
G03AA	*Progestogens and estrogens, fixed combinations*
G03AA05	ethinylestradiol + norethisterone*

ATC code	ATC group/medicine or item
G03AB	*Progestogens and estrogens, sequential preparations*
G03AB03	ethinylestradiol + levonorgestrel*
G03AC	*Progestogens*
G03AC01	norethisterone enantate*
G03AC03	levonorgestrel
G03AC06	medroxyprogesterone acetate*
G03B	**Androgens**
G03BA	*3-Oxoandrosten (4) derivatives*
G03BA03	testosterone
G03C	**Estrogens**
G03CA	*Natural and semisynthetic estrogens, plain*
G03CA01	ethinylestradiol
G03D	**Progestogens**
G03DC	*Estren derivatives*
G03DC02	norethisterone
G03G	**Gonadotropins and other ovulation stimulants**
G03GB	*Ovulation stimulants, synthetic*
G03GB02	clomifene
H	**SYSTEMIC HORMONAL PREPARATIONS, EXCL. SEX HORMONES AND INSULINS**
H01	**Pituitary, hypothalamic hormones and analogues**
H01B	**Posterior pituitary lobe hormones**
H01BA	*Vasopressin and analogues*
H01BA02	desmopressin
H01BB	*Oxytocin and analogues*
H01BB02	oxytocin
H02	**Corticosteroids for systemic use**
H02A	**Corticosteroids for systemic use, plain**
H02AA	*Mineralocorticoids*
H02AA02	fludrocortisone
H02AB	*Glucocorticoids*
H02AB02	dexamethasone
H02AB06	prednisolone
H02AB09	hydrocortisone
H03	**Thyroid therapy**
H03A	**Thyroid preparations**
H03AA	*Thyroid hormones*
H03AA01	levothyroxine*
H03B	**Antithyroid preparations**
H03BA	*Thiouracils*
H03BA02	propylthiouracil

ATC code	ATC group/medicine or item

H03C   **Iodine therapy**
H03CA   *potassium iodide**

J   **ANTIINFECTIVES FOR SYSTEMIC USE**
J01   **Antibacterials for systemic use**
J01A   **Tetracyclines**
J01AA   *Tetracyclines*
J01AA02   doxycycline

J01B   **Amphenicols**
J01BA   *Amphenicols*
J01BA01   chloramphenicol

J01C   **Beta-lactam antibacterials, penicillins**
J01CA   *Penicillins with extended spectrum*
J01CA01   ampicillin
J01CA04   amoxicillin

J01CE   *Beta-lactamase sensitive penicillins*
J01CE01   benzylpenicillin
J01CE02   phenoxymethylpenicillin
J01CE08   benzathine benzylpenicillin
J01CE09   procaine benzylpenicillin*

J01CF   *Beta-lactamase resistant penicillins*
J01CF02   cloxacillin

J01CR   *Combinations of penicillins, incl. beta-lactamase inhibitors*
J01CR02   amoxicillin + clavulanic acid*

J01D   **Other beta-lactam antibacterials**
J01DA   *Cephalosporins and related substances*
J01DA11   ceftazidime
J01DA13   ceftriaxone

J01DH   *Carbapenems*
J01DH51   imipenem + cilastatin*

J01E   **Sulfonamides and trimethoprim**
J01EA   *Trimethoprim and derivatives*
J01EA01   trimethoprim

J01EC   *Intermediate-acting sulfonamides*
J01EC02   sulfadiazine

J01EE   *Combinations of sulfonamides and trimethoprim, incl. derivatives*
J01EE01   sulfamethoxazole + trimethoprim

J01F   **Macrolides, lincosamides and streptogramins**
J01FA   *Macrolides*
J01FA01   erythromycin

J01FF   *Lincosamides*
J01FF01   clindamycin

ATC code	ATC group/medicine or item
J01G	**Aminoglycoside antibacterials**
J01GA	*Streptomycins*
J01GA01	streptomycin
J01GB	*Other aminoglycosides*
J01GB03	gentamicin
J01GB04	kanamycin
J01GB06	amikacin
J01M	**Quinolone antibacterials**
J01MA	*Fluoroquinolones*
J01MA01	ofloxacin
J01MA02	ciprofloxacin
J01MA12	levofloxacin
J01MB	*Other quinolones*
J01MB02	nalidixic acid
J01X	**Other antibacterials**
J01XA	*Glycopeptide antibacterials*
J01XA01	vancomycin
J01XD	*Imidazole derivatives*
J01XD01	metronidazole
J01XE	*Nitrofuran derivatives*
J01XE01	nitrofurantoin
J01XX	*Other antibacterials*
J01XX04	spectinomycin
J02	**Antimycotics for systemic use**
J02A	**Antimycotics for systemic use**
J02AA	*Antibiotics*
J02AA01	amphotericin B
J02AC	*Triazole derivatives*
J02AC01	fluconazole
J02AX	*Other antimycotics for systemic use*
J02AX01	flucytosine
J04	**Antimycobacterials**
J04A	**Drugs for treatment of tuberculosis**
J04AA	*Aminosalicylic acid and derivatives*
J04AA01	p-aminosalicylic acid*
J04AB	*Antibiotics*
J04AB01	cycloserine
J04AB02	rifampicin
J04AB30	capreomycin
J04AC	*Hydrazides*
J04AC01	isoniazid

ATC code	ATC group/medicine or item
J04AD	*Thiocarbamide derivatives*
J04AD03	ethionamide
J04AK	*Other drugs for treatment of tuberculosis*
J04AK01	pyrazinamide
J04AK02	ethambutol
J04AM	*Combinations of drugs for treatment of tuberculosis*
J04AM02	rifampicin + isoniazid*
J04AM02	rifampicin + isoniazid + pyrazinamide*
J04AM02	rifampicin + isoniazid + pyrazinamide + ethambutol*
J04AM03	isoniazid + ethambutol*
J04AM04	thioacetazone + isoniazid*
J04B	**Drugs for treatment of lepra**
J04BA	*Drugs for treatment of lepra*
J04BA01	clofazimine
J04BA02	dapsone
J05	**Antivirals for systemic use**
J05A	**Direct acting antivirals**
J05AB	*Nucleosides and nucleotides, excl. reverse transcriptase inhibitors*
J05AB01	aciclovir
J05AE	*Protease inhibitors*
J05AE01	saquinavir (SQV)
J05AE02	indinavir (IDV)
J05AE03	ritonavir(r)
J05AE04	nelfinavir (NFV)
J05AE30	lopinavir + ritonavir (LPV/r)*
J05AF	*Nucleoside reverse transcriptase inhibitors*
J05AF01	zidovudine (ZDV or AZT)
J05AF02	didanosine (ddl)
J05AF04	stavudine (d4T)
J05AF05	lamivudine (3TC)
J05AF06	abacavir (ABC)
J05AG	*Non-nucleoside reverse transcriptase inhibitors*
J05AG01	nevirapine (NVP)
J05AG03	efavirenz (EFV or EFZ)
J06	**Immune sera and immunoglobulins**
J06A	**Immune sera**
J06AA	*Immune sera*
J06AA01	diphtheria antitoxin
J06AA03	antivenom sera*
J06B	**Immunoglobulins**
J06BA	*immunoglobulin, human normal*
J06BB	*Specific immunoglobulins*
J06BB01	anti-D immunoglobulin (human)

ATC code	ATC group/medicine or item
J06BB02	antitetanus immunoglobulin (human)*
J06BB05	rabies immunoglobulin
J07	**Vaccines**
J07A	**Bacterial vaccines**
J07AH	meningococcal meningitis vaccine*
J07AJ	Pertussis vaccines
J07AJ51	diphtheria-pertussis-tetanus vaccine*
J07AM	Tetanus vaccines
J07AM51	diphtheria-tetanus vaccine*
J07AN	Tuberculosis vaccines
J07AN01	BCG vaccine*
J07AP	typhoid vaccine
J07B	**Viral vaccines**
J07BB	influenza vaccine
J07BC	Hepatitis vaccines
J07BC01	hepatitis B vaccine
J07BD	Measles vaccine*
J07BD52	measles-mumps-rubella vaccine*
J07BF	poliomyelitis vaccine
J07BG	rabies vaccine
J07BJ	rubella vaccine
J07BL	yellow fever vaccine
L	**ANTINEOPLASTIC AND IMMUNOMODULATING AGENTS**
L01	**Antineoplastic agents**
L01A	**Alkylating agents**
L01AA	Nitrogen mustard analogues
L01AA01	cyclophosphamide
L01AA02	chlorambucil
L01AA05	chlormethine
L01AX	Other alkylating agents
L01AX04	dacarbazine
L01B	**Antimetabolites**
L01BA	Folic acid analogues
L01BA01	methotrexate
L01BB	Purine analogues
L01BB02	mercaptopurine
L01BC	Pyrimidine analogues
L01BC01	cytarabine
L01BC02	fluorouracil

ATC code	ATC group/medicine or item
L01C	**Plant alkaloids and other natural products**
L01CA	*Vinca alkaloids and analogues*
L01CA01	vinblastine
L01CA02	vincristine
L01CB	*Podophyllotoxin derivatives*
L01CB01	etoposide
L01D	**Cytotoxic antibiotics and related substances**
L01DA	*Actinomycines*
L01DA01	dactinomycin
L01DB	*Anthracyclines and related substances*
L01DB01	doxorubicin
L01DB02	daunorubicin
L01DC	*Other cytotoxic antibiotics*
L01DC01	bleomycin
L01X	**Other antineoplastic agents**
L01XA	*Platinum compounds*
L01XA01	cisplatin
L01XB	*Methylhydrazines*
L01XB01	procarbazine
L01XX	*Other antineoplastic agents*
L01XX02	asparaginase
L02	**Endocrine therapy**
L02B	**Hormone antagonists and related agents**
L02BA	*Anti-estrogens*
L02BA01	tamoxifen
L04	**Immunosuppressive agents**
L04A	**Immunosuppressive agents**
L04AA	*Selective immunosuppressive agents*
L04AA01	ciclosporin
L04AX	*Other immunosuppressive agents*
L04AX01	azathioprine
M	**MUSCULO-SKELETAL SYSTEM**
M01	**Antiinflammatory and antirheumatic products**
M01A	**Antiinflammatory and antirheumatic products, non-steroids**
M01AE	*Propionic acid derivatives*
M01AE01	ibuprofen
M01C	**Specific antirheumatic agents**
M01CC	*Penicillamine and similar agents*
M01CC01	penicillamine

ATC code	ATC group/medicine or item
M03	**Muscle relaxants**
M03A	**Muscle relaxants, peripherally acting agents**
M03AA	*Curare alkaloids*
M03AA01	alcuronium
M03AB	*Choline derivatives*
M03AB01	suxamethonium
M03AC	*Other quaternary ammonium compounds*
M03AC03	vecuronium
M04	**Antigout preparations**
M04A	**Antigout preparations**
M04AA	*Preparations inhibiting uric acid production*
M04AA01	allopurinol
M04AC	*Preparations with no effect on uric acid metabolism*
M04AC01	colchicine
N	**NERVOUS SYSTEM**
N01	**Anesthetics**
N01A	**Anesthetics, general**
N01AA	*Ethers*
N01AA01	ether, anaesthetic*
N01AB	*Halogenated hydrocarbons*
N01AB01	halothane
N01AF	*Barbiturates, plain*
N01AF03	thiopental
N01AX	*Other general anesthetics*
N01AX03	ketamine
N01AX13	nitrous oxide
N01B	**Anesthetics, local**
N01BB	*Amides*
N01BB01	bupivacaine
N01BB02	lidocaine
N01BB52	lidocaine + epinephrine (adrenaline)*
N02	**Analgesics**
N02A	**Opioids**
N02AA	*Natural opium alkaloids*
N02AA01	morphine
N02AB	*Phenylpiperidine derivatives*
N02AB02	pethidine
N02B	**Other analgesics and antipyretics**
N02BA	*Salicylic acid and derivatives*
N02BA01	acetylsalicylic acid
N02BE	*Anilides*
N02BE01	paracetamol

ATC code	ATC group/medicine or item
N02C	**Antimigraine preparations**
N02CA	*Ergot alkaloids*
N02CA02	ergotamine
N03	**Antiepileptics**
N03A	**Antiepileptics**
N03AA	*Barbiturates and derivatives*
N03AA02	phenobarbital
N03AB	*Hydantoin derivatives*
N03AB02	phenytoin
N03AD	*Succinimide derivatives*
N03AD01	ethosuximide
N03AE	*Benzodiazepine derivatives*
N03AE01	clonazepam
N03AF	*Carboxamide derivatives*
N03AF01	carbamazepine
N03AG	*Fatty acid derivatives*
N03AG01	valproic acid
N04	**Anti-parkinson drugs**
N04A	**Anticholinergic agents**
N04AA	*Tertiary amines*
N04AA02	biperiden
N04B	**Dopaminergic agents**
N04BA	*Dopa and dopa derivatives*
N04BA02	levodopa + carbidopa*
N05	**Psycholeptics**
N05A	**Antipsychotics**
N05AA	*Phenothiazines with aliphatic side-chain*
N05AA01	chlorpromazine
N05AB	*Phenothiazines with piperazine structure*
N05AB02	fluphenazine
N05AD	*Butyrophenone derivatives*
N05AD01	haloperidol
N05AN	*Lithium*
N05AN01	lithium carbonate*
N05B	**Anxiolytics**
N05BA	*Benzodiazepine derivatives*
N05BA01	diazepam
N05C	**Hypnotics and sedatives**
N05CC	*Aldehydes and derivatives*
N05CC01	chloral hydrate

ATC code	ATC group/medicine or item
N06	**Psychoanaleptics**
N06A	**Antidepressants**
N06AA	*Non-selective monoamine reuptake inhibitors*
N06AA04	clomipramine
N06AA09	amitriptyline
N07	**Other nervous system drugs**
N07A	**Parasympathomimetics**
N07AA	*Anticholinesterases*
N07AA01	neostigmine
N07AA02	pyridostigmine
P	**ANTIPARASITIC PRODUCTS, INSECTICIDES AND REPELLENTS**
P01	**Antiprotozoals**
P01A	**Agents against amoebiasis and other protozoal diseases**
P01AB	*Nitroimidazole derivatives*
P01AB01	metronidazole
P01AC	*Dichloroacetamide derivatives*
P01AC01	diloxanide
P01B	**Antimalarials**
P01BA	*Aminoquinolines*
P01BA01	chloroquine
P01BA03	primaquine
P01BB	*Biguanides*
P01BB01	proguanil
P01BC	*Methanolquinolines*
P01BC01	quinine
P01BC02	mefloquine
P01BD	*Diaminopyrimidines*
P01BD01	pyrimethamine
P01BD51	sulfadoxine + pyrimethamine*
P01BE	*Artemisinin and derivatives*
P01BE02	artemether
P01BE03	artesunate
P01BE52	artemether + lumefantrine*
P01C	**Agents against leishmaniasis and trypanosomiasis**
P01CA	*Nitroimidazole derivatives*
P01CA02	benznidazole
P01CB	*Antimony compounds*
P01CB01	meglumine antimoniate
P01CC	*Nitrofuran derivatives*
P01CC01	nifurtimox

ATC code	ATC group/medicine or item
P01CD	*Arsenic compounds*
P01CD01	melarsoprol
P01CX	*Other agents against leishmaniasis and trypanosomiasis*
P01CX01	pentamidine*
P01CX02	suramin sodium
P01CX03	eflornithine
P02	**Anthelmintics**
P02B	**Antitrematodals**
P02BA	*Quinoline derivatives and related substances*
P02BA01	praziquantel
P02BA02	oxamniquine
P02BX	*Other antitrematodal agents*
PO2BX04[a]	triclabendazole
P02C	**Antinematodal agents**
P02CA	*Benzimidazole derivatives*
P02CA01	mebendazole
P02CA03	albendazole
P02CB	*Piperazine and derivatives*
P02CB02	diethylcarbamazine
P02CC	*Tetrahydropyrimidine derivatives*
P02CC01	pyrantel
P02CE	*Imidazothiazole derivatives*
P02CE01	levamisole
P02CF	*Avermectines*
P02CF01	ivermectin
P02D	**Anticestodals**
P02DA	*Salicylic acid derivatives*
P02DA01	niclosamide
P03	**Ectoparasiticides, incl. scabicides, insecticides and repellents**
P03A	**Ectoparasiticides, incl. scabicides**
P03AC	*Pyrethrines, incl. synthetic compounds*
P03AC04	permethrin
P03AX	*Other ectoparasiticides, incl. scabicides*
P03AX01	benzyl benzoate
P03B	**Insecticides and repellents**
P03BX	*Other insecticides and repellents*
P03BX01	diethyltoluamide
R	**RESPIRATORY SYSTEM**
R03	**Drugs for obstructive airway diseases**
R03A	**Adrenergics, inhalants**
R03AC	*Selective beta-2-adrenoreceptor agonists*
R03AC02	salbutamol

ATC code	ATC group/medicine or item
R03B	**Other drugs for obstructive airway diseases, inhalants**
R03BA	*Glucocorticoids*
R03BA01	beclometasone
R03BB	*Anticholinergics*
R03BB01	ipratropium bromide
R03BC	*Antiallergic agents, excl. corticosteroids*
R03BC01	cromoglicic acid
R03C	**Adrenergics for systemic use**
R03CA	*Alpha- and beta-adrenoreceptor agonists*
R03CA02	ephedrine
R03CB	*Non-selective beta-adrenoreceptor agonists*
R03CB01	isoprenaline
R03CC	*Selective beta-2-adrenoreceptor agonists*
R03CC02	salbutamol
R03D	**Other systemic drugs for obstructive airway diseases**
R03DA	*Xanthines*
R03DA04	theophylline
R03DA05	aminophylline
R05	**Cough and cold preparations**
R05D	**Cough suppressants, excl. combinations with expectorants**
R05DA	*Opium alkaloids and derivatives*
R05DA04	codeine
R05DA09	dextromethorphan
R06	**Antihistamines for systemic use**
R06A	**Antihistamines for systemic use**
R06AB	*Substituted alkylamines*
R06AB04	chlorphenamine
R06AD	*Phenothiazine derivatives*
R06AD02	promethazine
S	**SENSORY ORGANS**
S01	**Ophthalmologicals**
S01A	**Antiinfectives**
S01AA	*Antibiotics*
S01AA09	tetracycline
S01AA11	gentamicin
S01AD	*Antivirals*
S01AD01	idoxuridine
S01B	**Antiinflammatory agents**
S01BA	*Corticosteroids, plain*
S01BA04	prednisolone

ATC code	ATC group/medicine or item

S01E   **Antiglaucoma preparations and miotics**
S01EA   *Sympathomimetics in glaucoma therapy*
S01EA01   epinephrine

S01EB   *Parasympathomimetics*
S01EB01   pilocarpine

S01EC   *Carbonic anhydrase inhibitors*
S01EC01   acetazolamide

S01ED   *Beta blocking agents*
S01ED01   timolol

S01F   **Mydriatics and cycloplegics**
S01FA   *Anticholinergics*
S01FA01   atropine
S01FA06   tropicamide

S01H   **Local anesthetics**
S01HA   *Local anesthetics*
S01HA03   tetracaine

S01J   **Diagnostic agents**
S01JA   *Colouring agents*
S01JA01   fluorescein

V   **VARIOUS**
V03   **All other therapeutic products**
V03A   **All other therapeutic products**
V03AB   *Antidotes*
V03AB01   ipecacuanha
V03AB03   sodium calcium edetate*
V03AB06   sodium thiosulfate*
V03AB08   sodium nitrite
V03AB09   dimercaprol
V03AB14   protamine sulfate*
V03AB15   naloxone
V03AB17   methylthioninium chloride (methylene blue)
V03AB23   acetylcysteine
V03AB26   DL-methionine*
V03AB31   potassium ferric hexacyanoferrate (II).2H$_2$O (Prussian blue)

V03AC   *Iron chelating agents*
V03AC01   deferoxamine

V03AF   *Detoxifying agents for antineoplastic treatment*
V03AF03   calcium folinate

V03AN   *Medical gases*
V03AN   oxygen

ATC code	ATC group/medicine or item
V04	**Diagnostic agents**
V04C	**Other diagnostic agents**
V04CF	*Tuberculosis diagnostics*
V04CF01	tuberculin, purified protein derivative (PPD)*
V07	**All other non-therapeutic products**
V07A	**All other non-therapeutic products**
V07AB	*Solvents and diluting agents, incl. irrigating solutions*
V07AB	water for injection*
V08	**Contrast media**
V08A	**X-ray contrast media, iodinated**
V08AA	*Watersoluble, nephrotropic, high osmolar X-ray contrast media*
V08AA01	amidotrizoate*
V08AB	*Watersoluble, nephrotropic, low osmolar X-ray contrast media*
V08AB02	iohexol
V08AC	*Watersoluble, hepatotropic X-ray contrast media*
V08AC02	meglumine iotroxate*
V08AC06	iopanoic acid
V08AD	*Non-watersoluble X-ray contrast media*
V08AD03	propyliodone
V08B	**X-ray contrast media, non-iodinated**
V08BA	*Barium sulfate containing X-ray contrast media*
V08BA01	barium sulfate*

* Medicine or item name differs slightly from the name used in the ATC classification system.
ᵃ Provisional code pending formal approval by the WHO International Group for Drug Statistics Methodology.

Alphabetical list of essential medicines (with ATC classification codes)

Medicine or item	ATC code	Page
abacavir (ABC)	J05AF06	54
acetazolamide	S01EC01	69
acetylcysteine	V03AB23	48
acetylsalicylic acid	B01AC06	60
acetylsalicylic acid	N02BA01	47; 57
aciclovir	J05AB01	53
albendazole	P02CA03	50
alcuronium	M03AA01	68
allopurinol	M04AA01	47
aluminium diacetate	D10AX05	61
aluminium hydroxide	A02AB01	62
amidotrizoate*	V08AA01	61
amikacin	J01GB06	76
amiloride	C03DB01	62
aminophylline	R03DA05	70
p-aminosalicylic acid*	J04AA01	76
amitriptyline	N06AA09	70
amoxicillin	J01CA04	50
amoxicillin + clavulanic acid*	J01CR02	75
amphotericin B	J02AA01	53; 76
ampicillin	J01CA01	50
anti-D immunoglobulin (human)	J06BB01	66
antihaemorrhoidal preparation: local anaesthetic, astringent, and anti-inflammatory medicine*	C05A	63
antitetanus immunoglobulin (human)*	J06BB02	66
antivenom sera*	J06AA03	66
artemether	P01BE02	77
artemether + lumefantrine*	P01BE52	55
artesunate	P01BE03	77
ascorbic acid	A11GA01	72
asparaginase	L01XX02	77
atenolol	C07AB03	58; 59
atropine	A03BA01	46; 48; 63
atropine	S01FA01	69
azathioprine	L04AX01	47; 77
barium sulfate*	V08BA01	61
BCG vaccine*	J07AN01	67
beclometasone	R03BA01	70
benzathine benzylpenicillin	J01CE08	50
benznidazole	P01CA02	57
benzoic acid + salicylic acid*	D01AE20	60
benzoyl peroxide	D10AE01	61
benzyl benzoate	P03AX01	61
benzylpenicillin	J01CE01	50

Medicine or item	ATC code	Page
levothyroxine*	H03AA01	65
lidocaine	C01BB01	59
lidocaine	N01BB02	46
lidocaine + epinephrine (adrenaline)*	N01BB52	46
lithium carbonate*	N05AN01	70
lopinavir + ritonavir (LPV/r)*	J05AE30	55
magnesium hydroxide	A02AA04	62
magnesium sulfate	B05XA05	49
mannitol	B05BC01	80
measles-mumps-rubella vaccine*	J07BD52	67; 68
mebendazole	P02CA01	50
medroxyprogesterone acetate*	G03AC06	81
mefloquine	P01BC02	56; 77
meglumine antimoniate	P01CB01	55
meglumine iotroxate*	V08AC02	80
melarsoprol	P01CD01	56
meningococcal meningitis vaccine*	J07AH	68
mercaptopurine	L01BB02	78
metformin	A10BA02	65
DL-methionine*	V03AB26	49
methotrexate	L01BA01	48; 78
methyldopa*	C02AB01	59
methylrosanilinium chloride (gentian violet)*	D01AE02	60
methylthioninium chloride (methylene blue)	V03AB17	49
metoclopramide	A03FA01	63
metronidazole	J01XD01	51
metronidazole	P01AB01	55
miconazole	D01AC02	60
morphine	N02AA01	47
nalidixic acid	J01MB02	51
naloxone	V03AB15	49
nelfinavir (NFV)	J05AE04	55
neomycin + bacitracin*	D06AX04	60
neostigmine	N07AA01	68
nevirapine (NVP)	J05AG01	54
niclosamide	P02DA01	50
nicotinamide	A11HA01	72
nifedipine	C08CA05	59
nifurtimox	P01CC01	57
nitrofurantoin	J01XE01	52
nitrous oxide	N01AX13	46
norethisterone	G03DC02	65
norethisterone enantate*	G03AC01	81
nystatin	A07AA02	53
nystatin	D01AA01	53
nystatin	G01AA01	53

Medicine or item	ATC code	Page
timolol	S01ED01	69
triclabendazole	PO2BX04^a	50
trimethoprim	J01EA01	52
tropicamide	S01FA06	61
tuberculin, purified protein derivative (PPD)*	V04CF01	65
typhoid vaccine	J07AP	68
urea*	D02AE01	61
valproic acid	N03AG01	49; 70
vancomycin	J01XA01	76
vecuronium	M03AC03	81
verapamil	C08DA01	59
vinblastine	L01CA01	78
vincristine	L01CA02	78
warfarin	B01AA03	58
water for injection*	V07AB	72
yellow fever vaccine	J07BL	68
zidovudine (ZDV or AZT)	J05AF01	54

* Medicine or item name differs slightly from the name used in the ATC classification system.
^a Provisional code pending formal approval by the WHO International Working Group for Drug Statistics Methodology.